FIRE-EATER

FIRE-EATER

The Memoirs of a V.C.

by

CAPTAIN A. O. POLLARD

V.C., M.C., D.C.M.

With a Preface by

MAJOR-GENERAL THE RT. HON. J. E. B. SEELY

P.C., C.B., C.M.G., D.S.O.

9th Thousand

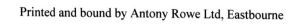
Printed and bound by Antony Rowe Ltd, Eastbourne

TO

MY MOTHER

AS REPRESENTING ALL MOTHERS WHO
WATCHED AND PRAYED WITH TORN
HEARTS BUT STEADY FACES WHILST
THEIR SONS WENT FORTH TO BATTLE

PREFACE

I HAVE read every word of this book, and I hope that thousands of others will read it too. In it is to be found the truth about men in the Front Line in war.

Just as books in depreciation of contemporary great men and great women are nearly always written by those who have never met them, even so is it the case that attacks on those who serve their country in close contact with the enemy are always written by those who have never been near the real Front. It has been my good fortune to survive through five years of war, much of the time quite near the enemy. As a result of that experience I wrote: " War is as ennobling to the actual combatants as it is degrading to the idle onlooker."

This book is a proof of that doctrine. Here is a man who gets to the late war at the first possible minute, who volunteers for every dangerous duty, who, as a private soldier, earns the respect and affection of all his comrades, receives the Distinguished Conduct Medal as an immediate reward for gallantry, and who finally earns and receives the most rare of all rewards for valour in the whole world, the Victoria Cross. But all through these experiences he is thinking of others more than of himself. Twice, after a desperate and successful hand-to-hand conflict, he returns to find a missing comrade. I myself saw one such episode in the late war. It is the hardest thing to do.

Some people think that these deeds of unselfish

courage are done by desperate men with nothing to lose. In my experience it is those who have most to lose who are the bravest in war. The writer of this book had everything to lose. He was desperately in love with the lady of his choice, and looked forward, as he tells us, if he survived, to years of incredible happiness. But when he learnt that this happiness was within his reach, it nerved him to greater unselfishness. One is irresistibly reminded, as one reads the modest but vivid account of the fierce engagement against a brave enemy which earned him the Victoria Cross, of Lovelace's famous lines :

> " I could not love thee, dear, so much,
> Loved I not honour more."

Every boy must long to receive the Victoria Cross. In this book he will learn how to deserve it.

John Bernard Seely

AUTHOR'S FOREWORD

THIS book is the account of my life from the outbreak of war in 1914 to the day I was demobilised in 1919. I have chosen a title which aptly expresses my attitude throughout the campaign. I enjoyed the War, both in and out of the line. Despite the discomfort and hardships of life in the trenches, I found pleasure in wandering about No Man's Land at night. " Going over the top " struck some chord in my nature which vibrated strongly to the thrill of the attack. Men called me mad. Perhaps I was. In this narrative I have endeavoured to set down a true account of my thoughts and sensations when going into action.

Many books have been written about the War, both fact and fiction. Those that I have read myself nearly all stress the sordidness and suffering which were inevitable in such a gigantic struggle. But there is another aspect of the picture which has not received the notice it deserves—the spirit of comradeship which pervaded all front-line troops ; the unselfishness with which men shared any extra comforts sent out from home with less fortunate comrades, or helped a weaker brother to " carry on." Many men gave their lives, generously and unhesitatingly, either to rescue or protect other men. True, they were often acting under discipline, but a high-minded spirit was there, or their efforts would have been half-hearted and the result a failure. The War is said to have brought out the beastliest instincts in man. It certainly brought out the noblest—self-sacrifice, unselfishness, comradeship. To-day, in peace time, we have men striving against one another for money and power. "Every man for himself and the devil take the hindmost" is the general slogan. It is not considered "business" to give a chance to an applicant for a job unless it is a certainty that he can "deliver the goods." He may have the responsibility of a wife and family and no money to supply them with necessities. That's his affair. If he has fallen in the race for success no one has time to stop and help him rise. He must be trampled underfoot. There is no parallel in commerce with a soldier risking his life to succour a wounded comrade.

If we had more of the spirit exhibited by Tommy when up against it, in dealing with post-war problems, the task would be easier, the achievement infinitely greater. Difficulties would be swept away by a tide of humanity actuated by the will to win through. The *motif* of this book is to show what that spirit was that bound together the British Army and made it possible for them to ignore defeat and gradually wear down the resistance of the toughest troops they have ever been up against in the history of the Nation. The story has naturally to centre round myself, although I would have preferred to have been able to write it in the third person. The thoughts and impressions are mine and are intended to point out a lesson that war taught us —that, as a Nation, we can accomplish anything so long as we work together. Nobody wants another war. All the glamour and romance cannot make up for the misery occasioned by the terrible loss of life. The fact still remains that those who gave their glorious lives in the defence of the British Empire, gave them in vain unless the Nation profits by their sacrifice.

CONTENTS

BOOK ONE

PREPARATION

BOOK TWO

FULFILMENT

15

Book Three

AFTERWARDS

BOOK ONE

PREPARATION

CHAPTER ONE

I JOIN THE ARMY

THE morning of the 30th April, 1917, was bright and sunny. I was awakened at ten o'clock from a deep refreshing sleep by " Bun " Morphy, at that time second in command of the battalion, who burst into my tent in a state of the deepest agitation.

" Get up at once, Pollard ! " he called in his rich Irish brogue. " The Divisional General wants to have a word with you ! "

I rolled over in my flea-bag and smiled up at him. Bun was a favourite with all of us.

" I'm afraid he'll have to wait," I rejoined. " I can't possibly get up at present. I haven't any pyjamas on."

It was lamentable, but it was true. We were lying under canvas at St. Nicholas on the outskirts of Arras, having only arrived from the line at three o'clock that morning after sixteen days in action. We were all dead tired. Our spell " up the line " had been particularly strenuous. In addition, I had picked up a slight dose of gas on the way down. Fritz was shelling the Arras–Douai road and I was too overjoyed at our relief to bother to don my gas-mask. The camp was a welcome end to a long march ; the Mess tent a pleasing centre. Several whiskies were needed before I fully realised I was back at rest. I was a bit tiddley-boo before I retired in search of my bed.

I found my tent all right. I found my flea-bag, properly laid out for me by my servant. The devil of it was I could not find my pyjamas. Perhaps I ought to confess that my search for them was rather perfunctory. I have often wondered why I bothered to undress. I had not had my clothes off for sixteen days ; one more night would have made very little difference. As it was, I stripped naked and crept in between the blankets.

Bun was too excited to grasp the situation.

" Never mind your pyjamas," he declared impatiently. " The General's waiting for you, I tell you."

The General would have continued to wait as far as I was concerned. Fortunately he eased the situation by coming to my tent in person accompanied by Colonel Aspinall, his G.S.O.1. How should one salute a general when in the nude ? King's Regulations makes no provision for such a contingency. I merely sat upright and hugged my blankets to my chin. Bun clicked his shining spurred riding boots to attention.

" This is Pollard, sor," he boomed.

I realised the feelings of a rare specimen at the Zoo being shown off to two interested fellows. Colonel Aspinall fitted his eyeglass to his eye. The General held out his hand.

" I'm proud to meet you, Pollard. I've been hearing all about what you and Haine did yesterday and I want to tell you I'm recommending both of you for the Victoria Cross."

The Victoria Cross !—the highest honour that any citizen of the British Empire can achieve. For a moment the tent whirled round me, the pole and the seams of the canvas hopelessly intermingled with khaki and field boots. In a daze I accepted the General's hand, forgetting all about my nakedness.

" I—I'm sure it's most awfully good of you, sir," I stammered. All my life I've always stammered in moments of great excitement. "It's most awfully good of you. Er——" I was at a loss for words; then I remembered. "I'm frightfully sorry I can't stand up, sir. As a matter of fact I couldn't find my pyjamas last night and—er——"

Major-General Lawrie was a very tactful man. He appreciated my embarrassment.

"I quite understand," he interposed. "You've not had time to dress. Have your bath and we'll have a chat later."

He turned to leave the tent. Colonel Aspinall's eyeglass dropped with a faint click. I felt that he was smiling. A moment later I was alone with my thoughts. The V.C. !

Had anyone told me on August Bank Holiday 1914 that I should ever receive the V.C. or even the D.C.M., or even that I should ever be a soldier, I should have roared with laughter. At that date I was twenty-one years and three months old, a clerk in the St. James's Street Branch of the Alliance Assurance Company, and utterly irresponsible. My chief interests in life were Rugger in the winter, tennis in the summer, and dancing all the year round. Girls ? Of course. They added a spice to life in the same way that one uses salt to season food. With the exception of one, with whom I had believed myself in love from the age of eighteen, none had any influence over me. I invested the one with every feminine virtue and shut my eyes to the fact that her real self might fall short of the wonderful creature of my imagination. She was two years my senior and thought me rather a silly ass. Nevertheless, my complete devotion made me useful to her in the capacity of an errand boy. Later—— But I anticipate.

Our Branch at St. James's Street had a staff of twenty-seven, ten of whom were Territorials. Mobilisation left us short-handed. The official attitude was one of annoyance. No Territorials would be sent overseas—the War would be over by Christmas—and no one else could be spared from the office to take part in a protracted holiday, playing at soldiers and guarding railways.

I did very little work during that first week. Every time I could slip away from my desk I went out into the street and bought a paper which I devoured eagerly in the security of the basement. With an optimistic belief in the British flag, I expected to read that we were victorious all along the line. Instead, the news was guarded. The Germans were advancing through Belgium.

Every time I looked out of the office window, I could see the red-coated sentries parading up and down outside St. James's Palace. Once a day the new guard came marching behind the blare of a full brass band. The music and the tramp of feet sent the blood coursing through my veins. The voices of my ancestors were calling, calling. A poster on the walls of Marlborough House stated that recruits were needed.

On the Thursday evening I stood outside Wellington Barracks and watched a party of khaki-clad Guardsmen leave for the front. The crowd were cheering. I joined in, but my voice was choked and there were tears in my eyes. Tears of envy at their good fortune. How could I be left behind ?

Was it Patriotism that stirred me ? That is the name for it, I suppose, but what did I, a mere boy, know of the danger in which my country stood. Everyone took it as a matter of course that we should be victorious. There might be a few temporary reverses but we were bound to settle the whole business before Christmas at the latest.

The following day I applied to the Secretary in charge of our Branch for leave to join the Army. He refused, quite rightly from his point of view. I took the turn-down calmly.

" You'll always remember I asked you, sir," I remarked enigmatically as I left his room.

He did not enquire what I meant. Possibly he thought I had asked to salve my conscience.

At five o'clock that evening I left the office never to return. It was a bold step to take. Had the War finished by Christmas, I should have been out of a job. Not that that would have worried me. I was already tired of life as a clerk and was contemplating emigrating to Canada. The opportunity of freedom from the slavery of desk routine was probably almost as big a contributory factor as Patriotism in the shaping of my destiny.

My choice of regiment was influenced by the fact that my only brother, four years my senior, had been a member of the Honourable Artillery Company for some seven years. I presented myself at the gates of Armoury House at nine o'clock the following morning. A small knot of men bent on the same errand was standing gazing at a notice pinned to the wall. It was to the effect that no more recruits were required. I waited for nearly three hours. Most of my companions went away to try other centres. A streak of determination in my nature, or should I more correctly term it obstinacy, kept me where I was. A man I knew, Malcolm Lewis, a member of our local tennis club, kept me company. At eleven-thirty our patience was rewarded. Someone came to the gate and said that recruiting had recommenced. I don't remember who it was or even what he looked like. I pushed and shoved to get inside. Malcolm and I ran the two hundred yards to the main building. An hour later we had passed the doctor, been attested, and were in the Army. Hurrah !

On Sunday morning I put a few things in a suitcase and took up my permanent abode at Armoury House. There was no real necessity for such a step but I wanted to be on the spot. I had cleared my first fence; my second was to get to the front. How was I to know that some special despatches might not be required to be taken overseas without warning. The H.A.C. might be asked to supply a messenger on the spur of the moment. I was there if needed.

Nothing so romantic came my way. Monday morning found me being initiated into the elements of drill. " Right turn by numbers—One !—Two ! " It was hot and tiring work but I was in the Army. What did I care ! There was never enough drill for me. I wanted to be efficient, to know everything. Potato-peeling, barrack-sweeping, and other fatigues chafed me terribly. They were necessary but they were not getting on with the job.

Route marches were rather fun. We used to march round the London streets and through the parks. Everybody sang. Sometimes we all sang the same song at the same time, but not often. There were usually several different songs going on at once. The result must have been ear shattering to the people we passed. One day we started off a different way. That in itself was an event. But a rumour passed down the line that we were going to the Tower to get our rifles. I squared my shoulders and held myself very erect. My ambition was getting nearer fulfilment.

The rifles were of an old pattern which had been discarded in the Army for years. But they were rifles. Handling mine for the first time gave me a thrill which is with me to this day. I was armed. It was a weapon designed to kill. I wanted to kill—not because I hated the enemy but because the primitive instinct was strong in me to fight.

A bayonet was supplied with the rifle. How many times I examined that bayonet in secret, feeling its edge and gloating over it. The desire to get to the front had become an obsession.

It was about this time that I first came into
prominence with the authorities. We had reached the
stage where we formed up as a battalion every morning
for the Commanding Officer's parade. The roll was
called and a report of the numbers of those sick and
on fatigue made to the Adjutant. One morning, one
man was missing—my brother. Imagine the consternation and excitement !

I was called out of the ranks and taken up in front
of the Adjutant, Captain Douglas. He was a tall man
of the superlatively thin type, and looked as though he
never had enough to eat. Khaki and standing at
attention increased the gauntness of his figure. Some
wag christened him " The Pull-through." The like-
ness to the brass weight on the end of a cord with
which one cleans the barrel of a rifle was unmistak-
able. The nickname has remained with him to this
day.

He eyed me sternly, to my secret amusement.

" Where's your brother, Pollard ? " he asked. His
voice was high-pitched, thin and throaty.

" I've no idea, sir," I replied. It was quite true.

I don't think he believed me.

" Are you quite sure of that ? "

" Quite sure, sir."

" Very well. You may fall in."

I fell in.

The same pantomime was repeated every morning.
At the end of seven days my brother was posted as a
deserter and I had achieved fame. I was the brother
of the only deserter there had ever been in the history
of the oldest Regiment in the British Army. What
a distinction !

I stuck strictly to my statement that I had no
knowledge of my brother's whereabouts, although it
only remained truth for the first two days. My brother
had deserted. Like me he was possessed with an

obsession to get to the front. He did not believe the Territorials would be sent overseas, so he deserted and enlisted in the Grenadier Guards under the name of Frank Tompson. He was my only brother, four years older than me, one of the finest athletes I have ever come across. I had spent a lifetime worshipping his exploits. No torture that has ever been invented would have dragged his secret from me.

Towards the end of August, our Colonel, the Earl of Denbigh and Desmond, paid us a visit. The Regiment was formed up in a square whilst he harangued us. At the end of his speech he called for volunteers who were willing to go to the front. I fully expected the response to be unanimous. I could not understand that everybody was not filled with the same fever as myself. If they did not want to fight, why the deuce were they in khaki!

Forty-two per cent expressed their willingness to serve. The following day the sheep were separated from the goats. The first battalion came into being. We were organised into companies, platoons and sections. I found myself in Number Eight Section of Number Ten Platoon in Number C Company. With me was Malcolm Lewis with whom I joined. My section commander was Sergeant John Pritchard, a great friend of my brother's. The rest of the section were strangers to me.

That very first morning I made two lifelong friends. How it came about I have no idea, unless it is that like attracts like. Harry Hoblyn was as big a fellow as myself. He had a merry twinkle in his brown eyes and a heart of gold. Ernest Chaland was the product of a French father and an English mother. He could speak either language equally fluently, an asset of the greatest value to us when we eventually found ourselves in France. From the first day we became inseparable —very shortly afterwards we were known as the Trinity.

Even the boldest of the non-commissioned officers treated us with respect.

More route marches, more drills, weird evolutions which seemed to have no purpose. Officers grew purple in the face, sergeants bellowed. Everybody took everything with the utmost seriousness. If we could keep a straight line when advancing in column of companies, there was not the slightest doubt we should be able to hold our own in a hand-to-hand conflict. In my simplicity I believed we should have got on better if we had paid more attention to understanding our rifles, but I was not yet in a position to voice my theories. Later—— But again I anticipate.

It was ordained that we should go into camp at Aveley in Essex on the 12th September. It was a red-letter day. We started with an inspection by our Captain-General and Colonel, His Majesty the King. After the review we marched through the City behind our brass band with fixed bayonets glinting in the sun, an ancient privilege which we hold as the City guard. The Lord Mayor took the salute as we passed the Mansion House. Our destination was St. Pancras, where we took train. A memorable occasion. It was the last time I saw London for ten months.

At Aveley we slept under canvas, a new experience for me. The whole of our section were in one tent and we began to find out each other's various idiosyncrasies.

Aveley is within an easy march of the Pirbright ranges and we spent an exciting day on our first practice shoot. Each of us fired a total of fifteen rounds. To me it was the most exhilarating experience of my life. Every time I looked along the sights I saw a German. Already I hated the whole German nation, for no other reason than that they were our enemies. My aim was deadly and I was complimented by our platoon sergeant, Sergeant Harrap, on it.

We should, no doubt, have acquired proficiency as

infantry soldiers by easy stages had our original programme been followed. But the arrival of a telegram from the War Office changed our whole outlook. We were ordered to proceed to France immediately. How we cheered. How my heart swelled within me. France ! The front line ! War !

The whole camp was thrown into a turmoil. Excitement followed excitement. There were a thousand of us and only eight hundred were to be taken. Who would be left behind ?

In our section the Trinity made the necessary selection. Sergeant Pritchard made a point of consulting us. Already we were making ourselves felt.

Another incident serves to show our growing power. The camp was surrounded by a high wall. The village which lay outside was out of bounds. The Trinity were thirsty. The Trinity decided to have a drink to celebrate our departure to the front. Walls were built to be scaled. The village boasted only one pub. Several sergeants, privileged people, were enjoying themselves when we arrived. No one took any notice of us. We left at closing time.

At dawn on the 18th September we fell in and marched to the train which was to take us to Southampton. Eight hundred of us, every man a Public School boy. Our average height was five feet ten. Without a doubt we were the finest battalion that ever crossed the water. Every man was a potential officer. Later when the country needed officers of the right type, the War Office realised the error of using such material as that which composed the first battalion of the Honourable Artillery Company as ordinary soldiers. Hundreds were killed as privates who could have commanded companies from the first day they joined.

I had not seen my people since we left London. There was no time to say good-bye. I scribbled a note in the train and threw it out as we passed through a station, addressed to my mother. It reached its destination.

Neither had I seen the lady of my dreams. She was away in the country visiting friends and had no idea of the sentiment with which I surrounded her. I was a knight going on a crusade. She was my ever gentle lady. I carried her favour in the form of a lace handkerchief of hers which I had stolen.

At Southampton we embarked on the S.S. *Westmeath*, an old tramp steamer that had been employed in bringing live cattle from Australia. We slept between decks in the cattle stalls. The odour was powerful. What did I care. She might have been a first-class liner. She was carrying me nearer to my ambition. I was *en route* for France.

CHAPTER TWO

I EXPERIENCE SHELL-FIRE

GOOD-bye, England! We steamed slowly down
Southampton Water whilst the shipping piped
Pip, Pip, Hurrah! on their sirens. With a top
speed of eight knots, we plunged and rolled our way
down the Channel, round Cape Ushant to St. Nazaire.
The ports on the north of France were still closed from
the scare of von Kluck's great flanking push.

I had visions of our plunging off the ship's side and
going straight into action. Instead, we marched through
the quaint French port to the British Camp. Accommodation was limited, and we were herded twenty-two in a
tent. The Trinity were the only three in our tent who
had the sense to keep our boots on. We were the only
three who spent a comfortable night.

The camp gave us our first intimate experience of the
British Tommy. We heard the most harrowing tales of
bayonet charges and hand-to-hand fighting from men
who had no more experience of war than ourselves.
The A.S.C. were especially bloodthirsty—in their
imaginations. We also heard the R.A.M.C. described
as Rob All My Comrades. It was unfortunately a true
tag—on occasions.

To my bitter disappointment, I learned that we were
not destined for the firing-line. The battalion was split
up for fatigue work at the various bases. C Company
went to Nantes, a delightful French town in the valley
of the Loire. Our camp here was situated in an orchard.

There was plenty of room, only five to a tent. The Trinity shared with Lance-Corporal Buster Brown, of Number Nine Section, and one of his privates, called Harwood.

More drill and more route marches. Our principal work, however, consisted of fatigues at the Army Ordnance depôt, where we were employed in loading trains with material. We all worked like niggers. We were doing our bit to the best of our ability.

The town was the greatest fun. Harry could speak French fluently, Ernest Chaland like a native. The townspeople were most hospitable.

One day they played a trick on me. We all marched up to the door of a fairly big house standing in one of the main thoroughfares. I thought we were paying a visit to someone of importance. Inside we were shown into a large well-furnished room. We all sat together on a Chesterfield and waited. After a few moments the door opened to admit half a dozen girls. All were stark naked with the exception of their shoes and stockings.

They paraded solemnly round the room to show off their points whilst Madame, their keeper, invited us to make our choice. The one who appealed to me was a little brunette called Mugette. I said so to Ernest, who called her over. She came and sat on my knee. Then she kissed me. It was very nice.

Closer inspection revealed a scar above her left breast. I asked her what it was; Chaland interpreted. She shrugged her dainty shoulders and said that a horrid drunken soldier had bitten her there in an abandonment of passion the week before. Two minutes later I was out of the house enjoying God's fresh air. I only visited one other brothel the whole time I was in France.

One of the duties we furnished was a guard over some German prisoners in the hospital. They were quite helpless, and our function was purely nominal, but it was a great joy to me when I was selected for the duty.

They were the first of our enemies I had seen and even to be near them gave me a feeling that I was nearer to the firing-line.

The guard consisted of three men and an N.C.O. On this occasion the Trinity succeeded in getting selected for duty together. We each did two hours on guard and then had four hours to ourselves. During the night, whilst off duty, I was having a prowl round to see what I could see when I came across a certain nursing sister. I will not divulge her name as she may still be in the Service. She was one of the red-caped regular Army Staff. She allowed me to walk round with her. Once I was able to help her with a refractory Tommy who had met with an accident whilst drunk. He was still drunk and Sister, who is little, could not quite manage him. I am big and could. Neither of us thought anything of the incident at the time. But I met her again in 1916 and she repaid me many times for whatever assistance I gave her.

All the nurses were nice. Two of them we met the following day especially so. Harry and I snapped at our opportunity and arranged a dinner for four. It was a great success. We spent the rest of the time we were in Nantes trying to get selected again for the Hospital Guard. We volunteered and tried to change with other fellows. Would the sergeant-major let us go? Would he hell!

He put us on another guard all right. Positively the most ridiculous armed guard I have ever encountered. Our job was to guard a mess of porridge. Porridge! Ye Gods!

The porridge was on the quay near the *Lousy Ann*, a corruption of " Louisaine," an old tramp steamer which served as the Military Prison. The porridge was for the prisoners and was prepared in a huge cauldron overnight on the quay-side. Our job was to see nobody had a dip into it.

The guard was deadly dull after the delightful society of the nurses at the hospital. Our only excitement was an estaminet near by. The girl who served the drinks was quite attractive and I attempted to improve my French on her. " Vous etes très jolie " was always a good beginning. I invariably used it to break the ice. She responded and we became as matey as a limited vocabulary would allow. I tried to tell her all about the wonderful girl I had left behind in England. To prove my devotion to the absent one, I showed her the lace handkerchief which I treasured in my pocket. She snatched it from me and refused to give it back. I can only think that I used the wrong words and she thought I was making love to her. In any case I must have reached the maudlin stage. Ernest tried to wake me when my turn came for duty, but I refused to come round so he took my guard for me. As far as I know, Suzanne still has my handkerchief. I never saw either her or it again.

Nantes was a very pleasant experience. I enjoyed it thoroughly except for the fact that I was the whole time in a fever of impatience to get to the firing-line before the War finished. We were moved at last. Orders were received for the whole battalion to concentrate at St. Omer.

The train journey occupied three days, so great was the congestion on the line. Most of the time we steamed at walking pace. It was literally possible to get out and pick flowers and still keep up with the engine. Train followed train at intervals of a few hundred yards.

We were lucky in being provided with ordinary third-class carriages. Most troops in France were conveyed in cattle trucks, forty men or eight horses to a truck. We were only eight to a compartment. By piling all our equipment in the middle, we succeeded in arranging two Bridge fours. We played all day and all night. There were no lights on the train, but we were able to play at night through my enterprise. The first evening we pulled into a siding at Rouen. The Trinity set out on a scrounge and I conceived the idea that if only we could pinch one of the station oil lamps our difficulty would be solved. The trouble was to get it out of its standard in full view of the railway officials. I solved the problem by taking the light from the station lavatory whilst Ernest and Harry kept guard. The difficulty was to convey it down the platform; it was very bulky. I managed it by taking off my coat and wrapping it round the brass container whilst Ernest carried the globe. We dared not light it until we were clear of Rouen, but afterwards it proved a great success. I still have it as a treasured souvenir.

St. Omer at last. British Army Headquarters. I began at once to feel we were really a part of the British Expeditionary Force.

The battalion was stationed in an old French barracks with the date 1815 over the entrance. That in itself was romance. Some of Napoleon's troops must have marched out through that gate to Waterloo. Judging by the condition of the interior the barracks had not been cleaned since. Rats abounded even on the topmost stories. The great compensation to me was that it looked at last as though we were going to do some fighting.

The London Scottish were also in the town. Like ourselves they had so far been engaged in fatigue work. Then one day they left in a hurry—for the front. Lucky devils! When would our turn come?

More drill, more route marches, more fatigues, more guards. The most interesting guard we furnished was at G.H.Q. Every man selected was over six feet. Harry and I were included when our company's turn to provide the duty came round, but poor old Ernest was left out. He was only five feet eleven. Harry and

I did duty together, one on either side of the gate. All the famous people passed us, including General Joffre. To ourselves we were all-important; to them we were just mechanical ornaments. Ever since that guard I have felt a strong bond of sympathy with the sentries at Buckingham Palace. How many of the people who pass them realise that they are capable of feeling and thinking? How many would be indignant if some of their thoughts were made public?

The day for which I had been waiting dawned on the 5th November. We all embarked in a fleet of London motor-buses and were driven to Bailleul. It had been in the occupation of the enemy only a week or so previous to our arrival. We were almost within range of shell-fire.

The Trinity found a snug little estaminet called the Café de St. Barbe. As usual, thanks to Ernest's Parisian French, we received preferential treatment from the barmaid. Here we came across some of the London Scottish and heard all about their recent experience at Messines. No doubt the story was somewhat exaggerated for our benefit. It filled me with acute jealousy. They had beaten us to a real engagement.

I hoped we should go into the trenches right away. I was once more disappointed. We set off to march down to La Bassée where we were to join General Willcocks' Lahore Division. We duly arrived. The General was quite courteous, but stated plainly that he did not want us. He wanted artillery. He thought from our title that we were artillery.

General Smith-Dorrien inspected us. Like everybody else, he told us we were a fine body of men. It seemed to be a sort of catchphrase at inspections.

The Lahore Division consisted largely of Indian troops, little Gurkhas and tall Sikhs. We heard that they were magnificent attacking troops but not too good in defence. They could not stand shell-fire; it was altogether outside their ordinary range of fighting.

We had our first experience of shell-fire here. We were employed to dig trenches whilst the authorities were deciding what they would do with us. Nobody thought to warn us that our task lay only just over a thousand yards from the front line. We set about it quite cheerily without taking the slightest precautions to make ourselves as inconspicuous as possible. The first day we were unmolested. The second, Fritz decided to give us a lesson. There came a noise like an express train travelling at an incredible speed. A metallic clap. A cloud of smoke billowed out a hundred yards in front of us, about fifty feet from the ground. A shell! High explosive shrapnel! A woolly bear, as this type was aptly named.

I leaned on my spade and watched, fascinated. I was really under fire. My pulses raced with excitement. A second shell followed the first. Then a third. There was a commotion a little way along the line. Men were running. Someone rushed by calling for the doctor. A direct hit. We had suffered our first casualty.

CHAPTER THREE

TRENCH LIFE IN 1914

AS a battalion, I think we were fortunate in our La Bassée experience. We received our baptism of fire and then had a few days to think it over. We had heard and seen shell-fire. It was no longer a vague, unformed threat. Another time we should have some idea what to expect.

Almost immediately we marched back to Bailleul. We were billeted in a school and for some unknown reason all leave was withdrawn. It might have been very irksome. Fortunately the Trinity succeeded in circumventing the orders of the authorities.

The school was surrounded on three sides by houses. The fourth, which gave on to the road, was protected by sentries. We waited until dark and then scaled the wall which separated us from somebody's garden. I went first. As I lowered myself on the other side of the wall, I found what I thought was a convenient stepping-place. It was actually a dog kennel. The dog, a large one, was inside. He came out with a rush and nearly had me. I jumped wildly into a flower-bed. His jaws snapped within a few inches of my leg. Happily he was on a chain.

Infuriated by his failure he made enough noise to wake the dead. His barking brought his mistress into the garden. By that time my companions had joined me. Ernest gave a fluent explanation. I heard the rustle of a paper note as it changed hands. Madame became all smiles. We followed her to the house, and tiptoed down a passage to the front door. It was necessary to tiptoe as we had picked out the one house where our company officers had established their Mess. We could hear them talking as we passed outside their room. It's an ill wind that blows no good. Had I not landed on the dog's kennel, we should have blundered in on them. The wine tasted especially good at the Café de St. Barbe that evening.

We left Bailleul to join the Seventh Brigade of the Third Division under the command of General Haldane. Our initiation into the mysteries of trench life was done by companies, each company going in for a twenty-four-hour stretch. The place chosen was Neuve Eglise, a quiet part of the line where the trenches were about eight hundred yards apart, too far for either side to do much harm.

Our turn came for the great adventure. We marched off directly it was dark. I felt no fear ; only a tremendous interest and excitement. The order came down the line, " No smoking and no talking." In dead silence we stumbled forward through the darkness. Dead silence except for the clinking of accoutrements. In the stillness of the night they sounded loud enough to be heard for miles. An occasional whizz-bang burst in our vicinity. After a while we entered a ditch. It was very muddy, and it seemed to me we should have done better to have stuck to the ground above. There was a halt in front and a long wait. Then a message came down that we were to take off our packs. The ditch was a trench and we had arrived.

Every third man was put on guard. When my turn came, I peered into the darkness with eyes that scarcely blinked. Every minute I expected an attack from the enemy. Well, I was ready for them. My rifle was cocked and fully loaded. I was determined to sell my life dearly.

Away to the left someone fired a shot. It was answered from the German trenches. At once everyone started firing until the night was deafened with the rattle of musketry. They must be coming. Star-shells, which both sides sent up at intervals, multiplied in number until No Man's Land was as light as day. I clutched my rifle and waited for the shock of the attack.

Gradually the sound of firing died away. Darkness descended once more. Sergeant Harrap came along the trench to see we were all right. We asked him what had caused the alarm. He laughed. Someone had seen something moving out in front. It was an old cow that had strayed to graze between the lines. Its temerity cost it its life.

After one or two such mild experiences of the front line, intermingled with various carrying fatigues, we began to feel our feet. Although some fellows began to realise they had chosen the wrong vocation in life, the majority of the battalion rapidly settled down to undergo the necessary hardships. I think we owe more than we appreciate to Colonel Treffry, our commanding officer, for the tactful way he handled the battalion at this time. He knew the type of men he was commanding —everyone was from a public school, delicately brought up, unused to roughing it. He insisted on our being broken in by degrees. There is not the slightest doubt that, had he allowed us to be pitchforked straight into the thick of things, we should not have given anything like such a good account of ourselves.

The trenches introduced us to a greater affliction than the most dangerous bullet that was ever moulded. Lice ! It was impossible to keep clear of them. They swarmed everywhere. To men used to a daily bath and clean linen they were like the torment of the damned.

At the beginning of December we began to take our turn in the trenches as regular infantry. We were working the F trenches in front of Kemmel. Three days in the front line and three in support. I well remember our first trip up there. Winter was upon us and it was bitterly cold. From Kemmel village we left the road and proceeded across country. Part of the way traversed a turnip field. I had been detailed to help carry ammunition for the Vickers guns. Two heavy boxes in addition to my rifle and ordinary equipment. Every time I stepped on a turnip, I slipped. Stray bullets from the German line hummed through the air. Once, whilst crossing a ditch, I fell. My outflung hand came in contact with a slimy something that gave to the touch. It was the face of a Frenchman who had been lying dead for some months. It was my first experience of death. I wondered whether it would ever be my fate to lie like that uncared for and uncaring.

The trench, when we reached it, was half full of mud and water. We set to work to try and drain it. Our efforts were hampered by the fact that the French, who had first occupied it, had buried their dead in the bottom and sides. Every stroke of the pick encountered a body. The smell! Ugh!

The cold was terrible. Standing in water as we were, it was impossible to keep warm. I kept beating my feet against the parapet to keep them from going to sleep. We lived for the rum ration which was all too meagre. I was in a traverse of the trench with the Trinity and "Scully" Hull. We swore that when we got out we would have a roast goose and a jolly good tuck in.

We were relieved at last and went back to the village of Locre. An enormous mail awaited us. I had several parcels in addition to numerous letters. My pals were similarly provided. The four of us set off to a neighbouring farm-house. Unfortunately we could not fix up the goose but had a couple of rabbits instead with potatoes boiled in wine. The farmer's wife brought the rabbits in alive and wanted us to kill and clean them, but although we were soldiers, that was beyond us. The rabbits were followed by plum-pudding and cake from home, also some mince-pies, chocolate and dates, and washed down with *vin rouge* and coffee. Some meal.

Our next turn up the line found us better armed against the elements. Mittens and scarves from home, spare socks, etc. I wore two pairs of puttees. Sammy (*alias* Ernest Samuel) discovered an old umbrella which was the envy of us all when it rained. The trench too was in better condition, the 1st Wilts having repaired it with sandbags. We carried on the good work.

The German trenches here were about two hundred yards away from us. The troops in them were Bavarians, magnificent fellows from a fighting point of view. They were mostly very good shots. Sniping became acute. The moment a head appeared above the parapet—zip ! came a bullet. We lost a lot of men this way in ones and twos. Being all in the neighbourhood of six feet, we needed a particularly deep trench.

Of course we retaliated. I used to fire an average of fifty rounds a day. Apart from everything else it was good practice. I had only fired fifteen rounds in my life before I embarked at Southampton.

The trench was provided with steel loopholed plates, through which we could shoot. They were really a snare and delusion. Several men were killed by a bullet coming right through the plate. I always used to fire round the side of a sandbag. After a few shots, when Fritz was getting on to it, I used to move it along the parapet a bit to a different place.

There was very little shell-fire. Fritz sent over a few salvos a day to let us know he was on the alert. They were mostly directed at Kemmel Hill on which were our Artillery Observation Posts. Our reply was ludicrous. I learned long afterwards that we were only supported by one 4·9 battery and a two-inch mountain battery.

We had absolutely no reserve of troops behind us except the half of the brigade which was supposed to be resting. Colonel Treffry once asked the Brigadier whether he did not think it unwise to risk holding the line with such raw Territorials as we undoubtedly were. I can imagine that the General shrugged his shoulders.

" At any rate," he said, " they would not run away. They would fight to the last man."

He was right. Not only the Honourable Artillery Company but the London Scottish and all the other Territorial troops in France had the guts to stick every hardship, privation or danger they encountered. They were the flower of England. In my own Regiment, every man was a potential officer. This was proved conclusively shortly after Christmas. The brigade was depleted of officers through casualties and sickness. The Brigadier called on Colonel Treffry. Twenty of our privates were at once selected and given commissions. After three months in France, without any additional training, they took their places at the head of regular platoons. In their privates uniforms, with only a star on their shoulders to distinguish them from their followers, they went straight into action. Every one of those men gave an heroic account of himself. One man from my own platoon, " Black " Scott, lies in a grave not very far from Kemmel. He was killed with the 1st Wilts. His name will be honoured for all time, not only in our Regiment, but also in the fine old County Regiment in which he lost his life.

In our Regiment the Colonel promoted several sergeants to commission rank. Many of our original officers had succumbed to the rigours of winter life in the line. Later officers arrived from England, some of them commissioned from amongst the people we had left behind. I fully realise there had to be some rule governing promotion, but I have always thought it a pity that seniority could not be given to men of experience.

A man who had served two months in France was worth five men fresh from home. Some of the later arrivals made good ; some were utter failures. The tragedy was that the failures drifted back to England, and because seniority was by routine, blocked the promotion of men worthier than themselves. I feel very strongly that this state of affairs should be made impossible. In war time, if for any reason a man is unfitted for his job, he should be reduced. My own experience was that the right men did the job whilst the failures, shelved of their responsibilities, held the rank and received the pay.

The idea of taking a commission had not yet entered my mind. I was quite happy in the carefree life of a private. My ambition to reach the line was satisfied ; a new one was born within me. I wanted to take part in an attack.

The trenches in 1914 were terrible. Sanitation was not yet perfected. Corpses, mostly French, were lying about unburied. Dug-outs were almost unknown. Those that existed consisted of a leaky lean-to against the side of the trench. We privates were exposed to all the elements.

Yet, in spite of all drawbacks, the life held a strong vein of romance. Men were drawn together in a bond of common sympathy. I have known men forgo the longed-for rum ration so that a comrade who was a bit under the weather might have a double dose. Everyone helped his neighbour without thought for himself. Death was opposite waiting for a carelessly exposed head. No one knew when his turn would come. War is said to bring out all the beastliest instincts in man. It also brings out the noblest. There was something almost Divine in the comradeship of those early days.

There was romance, too, in those long nights spent in the open air. One saw the moon rise and set in all its glory. It started as a ball of fire behind the German trenches. Many new soldiers out from England, on guard at night for the first time in the line, have called their officer's attention to a "fire behind the enemy lines." The fire, the rising moon, gradually turned to a ball of silver. Mounting slowly in the sky, it spread its radiance over the whole earth.

I have watched the stars twinkling in their myriads and wondered at the immensity of space. Face to face with the realities of the universe, I marvelled at the puny efforts of men to mould their destinies. Here to-day and gone to-morrow was brought home to me in a fashion there was no gainsaying.

Two hours on guard and four off was the order of the night. Every third man a sentry. On dark nights it was eerie work. I have stared into the darkness whilst the shadows moved and seemed to be creeping on me. I have been on the point of raising the alarm when my sinister crawling enemy has resolved itself into a bush.

We spent Christmas Day in the front line. At midnight on Christmas Eve we sang all the carols we could remember ; the whole company in one huge chorus. After we had exhausted our repertoire there was a lull. Then the Bavarians started in their trenches.

Christmas Day was uneventful. There was no shelling and both sides were unusually quiet. At noon the Trinity decided to let Fritz know we were on the alert and contemptuous of him. We climbed on to the fire-step and fired off five rounds rapid. There was no reply.

Christmas dinner consisted of bully beef and biscuits and Christmas pudding. The pudding was supplied by the kindness of the *Daily Express*. They were in tins, one between three men. We got a cup of hot tea to wash it down.

The cold was intense ; the ground was in the grip of a hard frost. We were only too thankful to be relieved. I felt curiously tired on our four miles march back to Locre. I staggered into the estaminet where we were billeted and collapsed on the floor, in the spot which had been my bed for the last six weeks.

The following day I was feverish; the stone floor became unbearable. Despite the extra blankets which Harry and Ernest unselfishly piled on me, I shivered unceasingly. There was nothing for it but to fetch the doctor. He pronounced jaundice and I was bundled off to hospital.

CHAPTER FOUR

I BECOME AN OFFICER'S SERVANT

THE hospital authorities sent me right down to the base. My heart sank lower with every mile the train moved away from railhead. I had failed my Regiment and myself. How often the Trinity had referred to some fellow who had gone down sick as a miker. How we despised those who had not the heart to face the dangers of war, or the rigours of the winter. Now my turn had come. I pictured my comrades I had left behind classing me with the fainthearts. Not the Trinity. They would never fail me. Nor would they allow my name to be besmirched. But there were others, men who did not know me.

" There's a fellow in C Company called Pollard who's gone down with jaundice," one would say.

" That's a good one," another would laugh. " How the devil these fellows manage to kid the doctor with these obscure illnesses beats me."

" I suppose he's gone to Blighty," a third would chime in.

" Of course, my dear fellow ! You don't suppose he's gone to all the trouble of contracting jaundice for nothing, do you ? "

Me. To be classed with the mikers. The iron entered my soul.

At the base hospital I begged the doctor not to send me home. He told me not to worry as there was not the slightest chance of him doing so. He examined my card. The word jaundice filled him with surprise. He told me I had no more got jaundice than he had. He spoke suspiciously. He seemed to think I had done something criminal by turning up at the base at all. He took my protestations for hypocrisy. My name seemed to be mud everywhere. It's a cruel world sometimes.

I was thrown out of hospital as cured, on the 4th January. I suppose, at the worst, I had had a chill on the liver. In the Army at that time one was either sick or cured. There was no middle stage of convalescence. The night I left hospital I spent in a cattle truck *en route* for Rouen. It's a wonder I did not get a fresh chill.

At Rouen I discovered our first draft of reinforcements. I was overjoyed. It would not be long before I was back with the Regiment. I was already an old soldier, someone superior to the new draft from home. They had to get up at six o'clock and parade. I felt that to do the same would be undignified.

The camp was a sea of tents. I discovered an empty one in a part of the lines that had been erected for troops who had not yet turned up. Diligent scrounging supplied me with three blankets. I was quite snug and lay in warm comfort each morning whilst the draft turned out in the cold. My breakfast, which I took about nine-thirty, I bought in the Y.M.C.A. tent. I missed all parades, all drills, all fatigues. I was unaccounted for.

I was discovered on the eighth day. The flap of my tent was torn rudely open about eight o'clock by the irate camp sergeant-major.

" So this is where you're hiding yourself, my lad," he said in a voice of deadly calm.

I ignored his unfriendly demeanour.

" Good morning, sergeant-major," I said brightly. " Do you want me for anything ? "

47

For a moment he could not speak. He grew more and more red in the face. I thought he was going to burst.

At last he found his voice. He was a regular soldier of the old school and he did not lack expletive. I should have wilted. Instead, he rather amused me.

I waited until he paused for breath before I ventured on an explanation.

"You couldn't expect me to know your camp regulations," I observed. "You see, up in the line——"

It was like waving a red flag in front of a bull. I knew perfectly well he had not been near the line.

"Don't you sauce me!" he burst in on me. "Report at the Camp Orderly Room at twelve o'clock."

With that he left me.

I don't know what dire punishment I should have received. I don't even know whether I should have been punished at all. I never went near the orderly room.

They say the devil looks after his own. I got in touch with the new draft after my breakfast as usual to hear the news. The first man I met told me they were parading at eleven o'clock to march to the station on the way to join the battalion. For the first time since I entered the camp I paraded with them. For all I know the camp sergeant-major is still looking for me.

It was nice to be back. It restored my self-respect for one thing. For another, I had missed my letters from home. They had been following me round from place to place. Now they would have a chance to catch up.

My mother was my most regular correspondent. She never failed me throughout the War. My friends were also very good to me. My chief delight at that time though, was that the one and only girl had started to write to me. She was very irregular, sometimes missing as long as a month or six weeks, but every time

48

she did write it gave me hope. Poor fool that I was. I read between the lines things that were never there. A phrase intended to cheer me up became an endearment. She had joined the London Hospital Staff as a probationer nurse. Heroine worship made her a second Florence Nightingale.

There were several changes in the battalion. The majority of our original officers had departed. In C Company all except the Company Commander, Captain A. Lambert Ward. Three of the sergeants were promoted. Monty (Vincent Montague), " Duggie " Davis and Laurie MacArthur. The fourth platoon was commanded by W. A. Stone, a new officer out from home.

Corresponding promotions were made from the ranks to N.C.O.'s and Harry became a lance-corporal.

A change was taking place in me at this time too. I crossed to France a mere boy, my outlook restricted. War was changing me into a man. I had not yet emerged from my chrysalis, but experience was making me more self-reliant. I began to realise the strength of my own personality.

" Duggie " Davis asked me to be his servant. I thought it over carefully. It would not make any difference to my going into the line. If it had I should have refused. On the other hand it gave me something to do when we were out as an alternative to fatigues. It also promised a trifle more physical comfort. I accepted.

I went further. A cook was required in the Company Officers' Mess. I volunteered and became the cook. I have never been able to decide why I took this job on. I knew absolutely nothing about cooking beyond such rudimentary undertakings as egg-boiling and rasher-frying. Somebody had to do it and I suppose I decided I would rather be poisoned by my own hand than by someone else's.

The Mess occupied a room at the back of the village grocer's shop. The proprietress was a dear old dame of sixty odd who lived alone with her daughter, a spinster of uncertain age. Fortunately for all concerned they could both cook well.

Being an officer's servant in those days was a rag-time business. I have never in my life been much good at getting up early in the morning. To have to get myself out of bed, prepare early morning tea for the Mess, rouse Duggie, brush his clothes and clean his boots and then cook breakfast was beyond me. Something had to go. The something was Duggie. I'm afraid he usually cleaned his own boots and brushed his own clothes. His bath I used to leave ready overnight. From Duggie's point of view I was the worst servant that ever happened. But, thanks to Madame, I was a very efficient cook.

After all, everything was on my side. It was impossible to vary the menu very much. Meat, when we got it outside a tin, invariably consisted of frozen beef. The only alternative was pork, which could be obtained occasionally from the local butcher. Otherwise my job consisted largely of wielding a tin-opener. And of course the servants had to come first. We took the pick ; the officers had what was left. I well remember one day I was standing in front of the stove cooking some succulent pork chops which I had wrested from the local butcher after a fierce argument. Laurie MacArthur, the Mess President, came into the kitchen rubbing his hands attracted by the appetising odour.

" Splendid fellow, Pollard ! " he cried enthusiastically. " It looks as though we're going to have a damned good lunch to-day."

I turned slowly from the fire, my fork poised in my hand.

" Yours is stew, sir," I gently disillusioned him.

He retired crestfallen. Stew from the Company cooker figured very prominently on the menu.

Of course the officers were very raw or they would never have stood the treatment we gave them. Later on when I held a commission myself, I was in a position to out-general my servant in all the tricks he tried on me. I knew them all so well long before he even joined the Army.

More promotions. " Fanny " Ward went up to second in command of the battalion. I was not sorry. Fanny was always a driver. His own personal courage was above reproach, but he never had the smallest spark of sympathy with anyone whose nervous system was not as strong as his own.

His place as Company Commander was taken by Captain Boyle, fresh out from England. Captain Boyle was the very opposite of his predecessor, a kindly personality who understood men and knew how to get the best out of them. He was the finest soldier we ever had in the Regiment. He never knew fear in any shape or form and always carried himself bolt upright in situations where most men crawled on their hands and knees. I gave him my allegiance from the first day I met him. His example and, I am proud to say, friendship made me into the Fire-eater I afterwards became.

The Mess gave a dinner to celebrate the change. The Colonel was invited and I was bidden to do my best. I promised a six-course meal and prepared some decorated menu cards. It was the best meal I ever served.

I started off with soup, followed by tinned salmon. Then came jugged hare perfectly cooked by Madame in the French fashion with prunes and things floating in a rich gravy. It was the dish of the evening. I made a rice pudding for a sweet. It was slightly burnt, but they couldn't expect everything. Sardines on toast made a savoury and I supplied a sixth dish in the form of dessert. The whole was rounded off with Madame's coffee.

I was called into the room to receive the Colonel's congratulations. I was so elated that I made them a rum punch. This was a great concession. They asked for their rum every evening only to be told firmly that there was no issue, out of the line. Needless to say, we had their portion to supplement our own.

Captain Boyle's advent made a great difference to our commissariat. He ordered all sorts of things to be sent out from the Army and Navy Stores. Tinned sausages, tinned plum-puddings, tinned cream, tinned cakes, tinned salmon, tinned tongues, tip-tree jams and other ripping things. From the first he announced that the servants were to have a share. Wise Captain Boyle. He placed us in a position which honour prevented us from abusing. It was all very well to help ourselves when the extras were forbidden, but it was a different matter when they were generously offered.

I was spurred to greater efforts and wrote home for a cookery book. It duly arrived. I opened it at the first page, visions of all the tasty dishes I would prepare floating in front of my eyes. The first recipe began, " Take a dozen oysters——" I opened the window and heaved the book across the street. The idea of taking a dozen oysters when one was in Locre in early 1915.

The culinary art was only difficult when I was out of the line. In the trenches I was an adept. My range of possibilities was so much more limited. It consisted almost entirely of warming up tinned food and making tea. Also I had fewer officers to bother about. Most of them were with their platoons. Duggie and I were nearly always with Captain Boyle at Company Head-quarters.

I was the reason for this ; not Duggie. The very

first night he was in a front-line trench Captain Boyle announced his intention of going out into No Man's Land to examine the barbed-wire entanglements in front of our trenches. He wanted someone to accompany him. I at once volunteered. After that I went with him everywhere.

It was very weird that first night out in front. There was no protection of any sort between us and the Hun. Every time a star-shell lit up the neighbourhood we had to stand quite still lest our movements attracted the enemy's attention. From time to time bullets whistled past us or thumped into the parapet by our side.

I was thrilled to the core. This was man's work indeed. I used to hope we should encounter a Hun patrol engaged on similar work to our own.

Captain Boyle spent a long time every night out in front. I think it soothed his great fighting spirit to feel he was exposed to certain death should we be discovered. To me those excursions were everything. The danger acted like a drug quickening my pulses. At last I was doing something worth while. I was as happy as a sand boy.

CHAPTER FIVE

SPANDBROK MOULIN

I WROTE the following letter to my mother on the 17th March, 1915 :

MY DEAREST MATER,

I expect you have been wondering why you have not heard from me for such a long time. The explanation is that we have been marooned in the trenches for the last twelve days and consequently have been unable to get any letters through. I have received the ginger-nuts and a splendid parcel from you and of course there are other things to come. The tobacco and the clean clothes. There were 337 bags of parcels when we arrived here—nearly half a bag a man. If I had not discovered a two-pound tin of tobacco in an empty châlet, I should have been left high and dry except for ration stuff. It was Benson and Hedges mixture of Bond Street. Goodness knows how it got there. I also found a statuette of Jeanne d'Arc which I thought of sending to you. I was afraid, though, that it would break, so I parted with it with regret.

War is changing from the slow monotonous round to attacks and counter-attacks now. One never knows where one will be next. I hear that all leave is stopped, so any slender chance I had has gone to the dogs. Still, there is a very strong rumour of our going back for a much-needed rest, which will be better than nothing.

Another parcel for me has just been brought in

containing clothes. Thanks tremendously. I took my vest and pants off this morning for the first time since the last lot of clothes arrived. I feel that this is rather a disgraceful confession to make, but really there are practically no facilities unless one cares to wash in water used by men from half a dozen different regiments with lice dead and alive floating on the top. Personally I chose the lesser of two evils, though now the weather is getting warmer I shall be able to have fairly regular baths in streams and ponds. I can manage to get my things washed all right and I am doing so, though of course handkerchiefs, etc., get so easily lost. Also, I am quite able to carry any amount of stuff now. You see, everything I do not actually want to carry about with me I put into my officer's valise. It is much easier like that as, of course, I do not want anything while in the trenches, except perhaps a spare pair of socks.

The line has been getting gradually more and more active all this month until now, what with shells and rifle bullets, going up to the trenches is like going out in a rainstorm. While leaving the trench with Mr. Davis the other evening, when we were only about two hundred yards from the German lines, a bullet hit the cobbles of the road by my side and the chips of stone flew up and hit my hand. Quite close enough to be exhilarating !

It was awfully jolly to have your letters delivered to me right in the trench. Our rations were brought up about two in the morning and I was asleep after an exciting day. An attack was delivered from the trenches on my right but was unfortunately repulsed owing to hidden machine-guns. Well, I was asleep at the bottom of the trench and woke up some time after and discovered two envelopes on top of me in your writing. Seeing double like that made me think I was dreaming until I opened them and then it was quite clear. Of course you can have my name stuck anywhere you like, only make sure first what they mean by a " Roll of Honour." " Rolls of Honour " are usually for people killed in action, so you can understand that I don't want to be shoved on that one.

By Jove ! Now the spring has started it does seem a shame to be at war. I heard a lark the other day singing like blazes and I knew perfectly well that if I stuck my head a foot above the parapet of the trench, I should have about ten bullets over. It seems so unnatural. Then I found a cowslip in a wood. The first this year.

Well, I must shut off now. The man whose block I am writing this on is cursing me for using too many pages. You will be glad to hear that I am as fit and strong as a two-year-old. We were relieved late last night and having a nine-mile march on top did not arrive here until three o'clock this morning. After I had arranged Davis's bed and given him some grub and incidentally myself too, and made a little hot grog and got to bed, it was a quarter to five. I lay down by the kitchen stove, and as the civvies are early risers, and of course lit their fire by the time I got up at ten, I was pretty nearly roasted. I woke up sweating with heat——

The rest is of an intimate nature with the exception of the postscript.

PS. Tell the pater that John Pritchard was shot through the neck yesterday. Fortunately it missed his spine and all the arteries. He will probably look in at the office when he has recovered.

The letter contains only the merest reference to the most exciting event, so far, of the War. " An attack was delivered from the trenches on my right——" We were not actually in it but we had a first-rate view of the whole affair which was the next best thing. A British attack ! How it stirred me !

The British position was on the slope of one hill; the German on the other. A shallow valley lay between. Our front-line trench was almost at the foot of the slope; the German being about two hundred yards distant and half-way up to the crest of the rise. The strong point to be attacked was called Spandbrok Moulin, nicknamed by us the " Moulin Rouge." Behind, in the distance rose the spire of Wytschaete Church.

Davis' platoon was in the support trench, a hundred yards or so behind our front line and almost on a level with the German front line. I was, of course, with it, and from such a position had a perfect view of the whole show.

The attack was timed for three o'clock in the afternoon, but owing to mist, it was postponed until later. It was preceded by a pitiable barrage of artillery fire which consisted of a few salvoes from our two batteries. Then a detachment of the Wilts swarmed over the parapet of the trenches on our immediate right. The attack was launched.

Poor devils! They did not get very far. The Huns, probably warned by our unusual artillery activity, were prepared. As the first of our troops made an appearance, the hitherto hidden shutters protecting four machine-guns which formed the armament of the " Moulin Rouge " were slid back. The guns opened fire. Nothing could live in such a storm of lead. The attacking troops went down like ninepins. One officer got about fifty yards. He was a big fellow and carried a rifle and bayonet which he waved over his head. Gallant fellow!

I ought to have been frightened. I ought to have realised the futility of infantry trying to cross open ground in face of concentrated machine-gun fire. I ought to have prayed that it might never be my lot to be sent to certain death on such a mission. Instead, my blood raced through my arteries and veins, and I was filled with such a rage as I had never experienced in my life before. The Hun became my enemy then. He was mowing down my countrymen who were helpless to retaliate. Had not the merest thread of discipline restrained me I should have leaped our parapet and rushed down the slope of the hill, the blood lust in my heart. As it was I rested my rifle on a sandbag and fired as rapidly as I could work bolt and trigger.

" Look out ! " yelled a voice. I ducked just in time. One of the enemy machine-guns was traversing our parapet. Plop-plop-plop-plop came the bullets in mechanical regularity. One struck the sandbag I had been using as an arm-rest and whined away in a ricochet. Plop-plop-plop-plop, the menace passed on its way. I was up again in a flash firing for all I was worth whilst the bodies of the attackers lay in grotesque heaps in front of me to urge me on.

I looked along our trench. Everyone was up on the fire-step firing, firing. It was the same in the front line. With a groan I realised it was all in vain. The attack had failed. The Hun was triumphant. The Moulin Rouge remained intact.

Later that night I tried to think out for myself how the attempt might have been made successful. Without the intervention of a miracle the place seemed impregnable. I suppose the theory held by Brigade Staff was that the artillery would have registered a direct hit or two on the machine-gun nest before the infantry advanced. Had they knocked out only two of the four machine-guns the assaulting troops might have stood a chance. German machine-guns were only able to traverse through thirty degrees without moving the carriage on which they were mounted. In normal practice they were arranged in pairs, aimed to fire at an angle so as to cross the fire of another pair placed further along the trench. In this way an effective screen was built up which protected the whole of the line with a hail of bullets. If one of the pairs got knocked out, the arrangement broke down, as a gap appeared in what was otherwise an impenetrable barrier. This apparent weakness in disposition was responsible for more than one Victoria Cross earned during the War. It was manifestly impossible for the bravest man in the world to advance in the teeth of a machine-gun in action, but he could move about in perfect safety outside its zone of fire, provided he was not fired on from another direction.

At the Moulin Rouge the artillery failed to put any of the machine-guns out of action and the attack was held up. To me the failure was a distinct shock. I had always believed British Infantry to be invincible ; to see them rendered impotent was a revelation which dismayed me. Their courage was unquestioned. My National pride swelled within me and a lump came into my throat as I remembered how those men had gone forward to their deaths. The officer who had shown so noble an example set me a standard which I kept in mind all through all the campaign. I should be proud to die in similar circumstances. What then was the cause of our reverse ?

Were the Germans braver than ourselves ? Certainly not ! The stories of Le Cateau and Landrecies told us that. Tales were rife of the German soldiery being driven forward to attack by officers stationed behind them with revolvers. Man to man we were infinitely superior ; in armament, we were sadly inferior. Artillery, shells, machine-guns, number of men in the field, we were outnumbered at every point. The odds against us were overwhelming. Nothing but indomitable British pluck pulled us through at this period of the War.

Of course I did not reach all these conclusions at this time. I got as far as realising that we were attacking up a hill to try and dislodge an enemy perched on the top with better weapons than we possessed, and then gave it up. But the affair of the Moulin Rouge made a deep and lasting impression on my mind. One lesson which I took to heart is indirectly responsible for my being alive to-day. I realised that bravery by itself is useless against modern weapons of war. Strategy and guile must also be employed to attain success. The most notable example of my putting this theory into practice was on the occasion of my winning the Victoria Cross. But there are several others when I appreciated the truth of the axiom that " Discretion is the better part of Valour."

Actions speak louder than words. I had taken part in many discussions about what various people would do in an actual attack. I now had an opportunity of seeing how far our estimates were correct. Some acted up to standard; others fell woefully short. Some, amongst whom were fellows considered weaklings, went through the ordeal cool and unruffled. Others, and I regret to say some we had idolised, became nervous wrecks.

Our officers naturally came in for most criticism. We learned which ones we could rely on when our turn came to make an assault. Captain Boyle was magnificent and enjoyed his afternoon as much, or more, as if it were a play. Poor X was bewildered, and although he had no fear for himself, developed a dread that he would be unable to lead his men across No Man's Land. From that hour his efficiency as a combatant officer was finished. Y was over-excited and I formed the opinion that I should not care to have to trust to his judgment in a crisis. I do not for a moment belittle his personal courage which was always above reproach. He was just too highly strung to have adequate control of his actions.

The following incident will illustrate my meaning. As soon as the attack was over, I turned my attention to getting some water boiled to make X a cup of tea. I was on my hands and knees attending to the stove when someone delivered a terrific kick to my posterior, nearly upsetting the whole outfit.

" Get up on the parapet, man ! Don't skulk down there ! What are you doing ? "

I swung round. Y was towering over me. His face was flushed and his eyes starting out of his head. His lips twitched and his voice was almost falsetto. I looked him in the eye.

" Making you a cup of tea, sir," I said quietly.

He made no reply but turned and hurried away. In his excitement he had at first failed to recognise me. Even in those early days I had achieved a reputation which was incompatible with cowardice. Later came an indirect apology. I was described as a splendid fellow for having the presence of mind to prepare tea when it was most urgently needed. But that was after the shelling had subsided.

Later that night I saw a remarkable demonstration of mind over matter. The signaller on duty in our trench in charge of the telephone was shaking like a jelly. He could scarcely hold his instrument steady to his ear. To watch him one would conclude that he was almost paralysed with fright.

Suddenly the line went dead. A shell had cut the wire. Without a moment's hesitation, he climbed the parapet and disappeared into the darkness in search of the break. His duty was to keep the line intact, and personal fear or no personal fear, his duty was carried out to the letter. I sometimes wonder whether sufficient credit is given to the signallers who kept communications open under impossible conditions, often in face of withering fire. Their job was of vital importance. They carried it through with quiet efficiency without fuss. Of their number, Evans was a worthy member.

The Moulin Rouge was a small affair in itself but it was a milestone in my career, which marked the formation of a determination to attempt to live up to the picture I had always had in my mind of what a British soldier should be. I resolved that no one should ever say of me that I flinched in face of danger. We had been shaken up and I realised I was as good as most men and better than some. Hitherto I had been content to do as I was told. From now on I would look for an opportunity to distinguish myself.

CHAPTER SIX

I AM PROMOTED

WE went back to rest the following day. The weather was getting gradually warmer with the advent of Spring and we were able to enjoy to a limited extent the glorious country in which we were operating. It was a strange contrast to watch the peasants ploughing in the fields and then climb up to the top of a hill to see the shells bursting in the distance in a long irregular line like waves breaking on the seashore. Everything was so peaceful in our rest billets, just like home, and yet, on the other side of the hills, thousands of men were engaged in mortal combat.

Our rest was of short duration. After only four days we returned to the line, though not to the same part of it. This time we moved further north to St. Eloi, and took over the " P " trenches. The Huns had broken through here only the Sunday previous to our arrival and the consequent reshuffling had provided some new trenches. They were very narrow and not nearly so comfortable as our old ones. Neither had they any shelters although some were quickly improvised.

It was in this part of the line that I made the acquaintance of two new weapons of frightfulness. Trench mortars and gas. The German trench mortar fired a projectile that looked exactly like a sausage. It consisted of a steel shell packed with 1200 pounds of high explosive. One could see them rise from somewhere behind

63

the enemy front-line trench and turn slowly over and over in the air until they landed and burst with an ear-splitting screech.

The first time I saw them used was against the 5th Battalion of the Northumberland Fusiliers who were immediately on our right. Fritz selected a piece of trench about four hundred yards long and bombarded it for about an hour. At the end of that time the earth was flat. The casualties were terrific and would have been even worse had not the majority of the Fusiliers been moved along to our trench. We " stood to," expecting every minute that the Hun would attack but for some reason he was content with his bombardment.

Gas was used against the Canadians who were holding the line just north of the Ypres Salient a few miles from us. All we knew of it was a faint sickly smell but we were very lucky that Fritz had not chosen St. Eloi for his demonstration. Within a few days we were served out with our first gas masks, gauze pads about six inches long and two wide which we were supposed to tie over our mouths and noses. From what I learned of gas later in the War they would have been totally ineffective, but, at the time, such is the faith of mankind, we believed them to be adequate protection.

We had returned to our regular four days in and four days out. The time out was spent at a town called Dickebushe, believed to be out of range of shell-fire. On our first visit I threw up my job as officer's servant. It was the effect of the attack at the Moulin Rouge that decided me. Something had come to life within me that had not been there before. I did not know what it was but was conscious of a feeling of restlessness. I felt I was not doing my full share to win the War.

The day I returned to the ranks, Captain Boyle sent for me and promoted me to Lance-Corporal. He told me I should have been promoted earlier had I not been in the Mess. At the time I did not mind very much. Not having tasted the joys of leadership I did not know what I had missed.

Even now the Trinity was not re-united. Harry and Ernest, who were both in hospital at the time I became a servant, had since returned to the battalion. Harry was now a sergeant and although we saw a lot of him, of course he could not live with us.

The disruption became permanent almost at once. The three of us were sitting in a room at the back of the local grocer's store one afternoon drinking champagne when a long distance, high-velocity shrapnel shell burst over the town. Panic and pandemonium ! The Germans were coming ! Such a thing had never happened before and the townspeople were shaken to the core. Harry felt he had better go out and see what was happening. Ernest and I stayed to finish the bottle.

The first shell was followed by a second and a third. The battalion was ordered to occupy some trenches behind the town. " Fanny " Ward rushing down the street caught sight of Ernest and me leaning out of the window and ordered us to join our Company. We went to our billet to get our rifles and by the time we reached the spot where the battalion was assembled the whole show was over.

We went in search of Harry and found him lying with a shrapnel wound in both legs. Several other casualties were with him. The shells had mostly passed over the town and burst beyond. Had the troops stayed where they were, no one would have been hit. As it was they ran right into it. Poor old Harry ! It finished the War for him. After a year in hospital he was discharged from the Army as his wound failed to heal. I met him quite recently and his wound is not healed yet. He has to dress it every day, sixteen years after he received it !

The Trinity was dissolved. Ernest and I had a day or

C

two on our own and then Percy arrived on a new draft from home. Percy Lewis was my greatest friend before the War. For years we were inseparable. The War came and I joined up. Percy tried to do the same but was rejected. He had chronic valvular disease of the heart. He tried every recruiting office in London and was consistently turned down. At last he wrote me he had been accepted in my own Regiment as A1 fit. I was naturally amazed at such a miracle until he let me into the secret.

It was so ridiculously easy that I wonder whether any other enthusiasts adopted the same wheeze. Percy got a friend of his about the same height and build as himself to present himself as a recruit in the name of Percy Lewis. He passed the doctor with flying colours and was duly attested and received instructions to report for duty on the following day. On the following day Percy turned up in person. In the rush of recruits passing through, no one noticed the substitution and Percy was duly drafted to the front, valvular disease of the heart and all. I always think of dear old Percy when some laddie or other explains solemnly how much he would have liked to fight for his country if only the doctors had let him. Where there's a will there's always a way. Percy's heart may have been physically defective but it did not prevent him losing his life in the service of his King.

We went up to the line almost immediately after Percy's arrival so we had no time to show him round our bit of Belgium beforehand. He certainly got a damned good initiation into war conditions. To start off we were in support to a minor attack which was carried out to straighten a bit of the front line. It was not nearly as exciting as the Moulin Rouge as we were entrenched in a wood and could not see what was taking place. As soon as it was finished, this time I am glad to say it was successful, we were employed on endless fatigues strengthening the front line. The first night we were split up into parties of six to carry railway lines a distance of about two miles. If anyone who reads this is fed up with normal slimming exercises I can strongly recommend carrying railway lines as the most awkward, damnably tiring and unpleasant job it is possible to undertake. Unless you have every one of the same height the tallest man gets considerably more than his share of the weight. Every stumble tends to break the shoulder-blades of the other five.

I thought that first night had finished Percy. He was whacked when we turned in but there was more to come. The next night we had six hours' solid digging, making a new trench about fifty yards behind the front line. The night after we went out again and filled it in as it was not wanted. I don't know how they trained our reserve battalion, but none of the new draft seemed to have ever done any digging in their lives. They soon learned though. No slave-driver's whip could be a more adequate teacher than the knowledge that a machine-gun might open fire at any moment.

We were still in the line on the fourth of May, my birthday. Owing to the transport being engaged in bringing up extra sandbags and barbed wire to strengthen the new position, our parcels were hung up for over a fortnight, although we received our letters regularly. I knew a birthday cake and other delicacies were on the way and was on tenter-hooks in case they got spoiled. To add to my tantalization a pal of mine in the transport reported that a monstrous parcel was waiting for me at the battalion post office.

Something had to be done about it. The question was, what? For two nights I argued and implored. At last he promised to see what he could do. My birthday arrived and slowly passed. Shortly after dusk the ration carts came creaking into the wood. With a great air of mystery my transport friend turned back the tarpaulin of his limber. The marvellous parcel was there. He had found the post office temporarily deserted and had slipped in and carried it off. That night Number Eight Section had a glorious feed. I was the only man in the battalion with a parcel and the envy of all outside my immediate circle. No birthday cake ever tasted more delicious.

What a change had taken place in my life in the space of a short year. I was now twenty-two and a veteran soldier, inured to gunfire and physical discomfort. Fit as a fiddle, I could handle pick and shovel with the best. But where was it all leading ? What was to be the final outcome ?

Already in eight months our brave battalion of eight hundred had dwindled to less than one hundred. The remainder of our complement had come out later on the various drafts. Of the originals, some had gone home sick or wounded, some had taken commissions, some were dead. What was to be my fate ? Into which category should I fall ?

Then there was the question of the termination of the War. Even in those early days one had a feeling of impotence. The lines seemed so vast ; the trench systems so deep. Every minor attack, successful or unsuccessful, seemed so futile. The only thing that one was certain of was that lives would be lost. Some ground might be gained but there was always another trench beyond.

Faith is a marvellous attribute. Wherever I went, whoever I talked with was certain that we should win. Even the pessimists croaked only of Germany's stubbornness in prolonging their surrender. How could they hope to defy us for more than a few months longer.

The fire-eaters were now few and far between. There was very little talk of bayonet charges and assaults. The general theme was leave and how to spend it. Some of us were still keen to go over the top, however.

Ernest's French blood made him desire to skewer a Hun or two. Percy only worried about his physical discomfort, and lack of the amenities of civilised life. He accepted shells and bullets with the sang-froid of a philosopher. Even Captain Boyle, fire-eater that he was, did not present a bolder front to the enemy. I never saw Percy duck or flinch even when a shell landed within a few yards of him. If crossing No Man's Land unarmed and strangling a few Huns with his bare hands could have brought the War to a speedy termination, and allowed him to get home to his own bed and board, Percy would have attempted the deed with the utmost cheerfulness.

I myself was as keen as ever to take part in a real engagement. True I should have welcomed a few days' leave to break the monotony of trench life. But only with a healthy youthful desire to have a good time. I also wanted to see my mother, from whom I had never been away more than a few days at a time prior to 1914.

Lastly but not leastly, I wanted to see Her whom I now, though without any justification, looked on as my girl. I suppose I possess a strong strain of romantic sentiment. I had heard from her about once a month—just friendly, newsy letters such as she might have written to any male acquaintance. In that womanless world of the forward area I had weaved into them thoughts they had never been intended to express. I persuaded myself that each wish for my health concealed a special meaning ; each box of chocolates or packet of cigarettes I regarded as a special token. I hugged her image to my heart. I was fighting for England, but now England was personified in her. She was my ever gentle lady, for whom, if necessary, I would lay down my life. I wanted leave. Yes, I wanted to go home and tell her of my love so that when I returned—and in my egotism, I had no doubt of her response—I should have the knowledge of our bond always with me to urge me to greater effort.

Twenty-two is an impressionable age. Had I been living a normal life at home, mixing with as many girls as men, it is probable that I should have got over my infatuation without difficulty. She had always been at pains to snub me before the War. No doubt she would have gone on doing so until I turned naturally to someone more responsive to my devotion. As it was, there were no other girls, if one excepts the Flemish peasants, who were certainly never attractive to me. I dreamed of her, the one and only, placed her on a pedestal, endowed her with all the virtues. Never was any girl given a truer or more whole-hearted adoration.

CHAPTER SEVEN

YPRES

THE first time I saw Ypres it was a busy market town, its streets thronged with civilians and soldiers. With the exception of some minor damage here and there, it was untouched. Ernest and I and two other fellows got leave to go over from Dickebushe for the day. The distance was about nine kilometres, a mere nothing to us without our equipment. The day was one of brilliant sunshine, and we set forth in the morning as happy as sandboys. To judge from our demeanour we might have been transported into another sphere, where war was unknown. The only reminder of our grim calling was the rifle which each of us carried slung over his shoulder. It was a regulation that no man should leave the vicinity of his unit without his " best friend." Each magazine was charged with ten rounds of ammunition—in case.

We only made one stop on the way out. That was at a small and dirty estaminet which reminded me of the inn just outside Postbridge on Dartmoor which Eden Philpotts describes in his *The Thief of Virtue*. Here we sampled some cognac distilled from potatoes, surely the vilest drink ever conceived by ingenious man.

We entered Ypres by the station, crossing the square which will always remain in my memory because it was here I saw the biggest shell-hole I ever came across during the whole War. It was fully sixty-five feet across, and about thirty deep. It is said that seventeen dead horses were buried in the bottom of its crater without making any appreciable difference to its appearance. The shell which made it was fired from a seventeen-inch gun, the one which caused such dreadful devastation in the town later on. On the occasion of this first visit, it had not begun its fearful work.

Happy smiling Ypres! The main square was packed with officers and men of the British, French and Belgian armies, jostling shoulder to shoulder with sturdy Flemish peasants and their heavy spouses, or stepping aside for dainty laughing maidens, exquisite sight for men who had scarcely seen a feminine face for months.

We spent the morning sightseeing round the ruined Cloth Hall, the ramparts, and other points of interest, And, of course, the shops. We had to visit the shops, not so much for the purpose of buying anything as to have a talk and a laugh with the girl assistants. It was all great fun.

Mindful as always of Her whom I adored, I took advantage of a few moments whilst my companions were engaged to slip away by myself. I wanted to buy her an extra special souvenir. Now, despite my eight and a half months on the Continent I could speak very little French. Either Ernest or Harry had always been at hand to interpret for me. On my own I was in a difficulty.

I chose a big emporium in the square and marched boldly up to the counter. A black-eyed, red-lipped houri smiled at me and demanded what I wanted. With the best accent I could produce I asked politely for "Du dentelle, s'il vous plait, m'mselle."

What an opportunity to have a game with the soldat anglais. She called up another equally charming conspirator, and between them they proceeded to show me tray after tray of the most ravishing feminine knickers. Some had small trimmings of lace, others seemed to be all lace. Some were kept up with buttons, others with elastic. Some were tight at the knee, others voluminous. In short they showed me every conceivable sort and type that was ever invented, the whole time shaking with merry laughter. Every time I expostulated or attempted to explain they shook out another ridiculous garment in front of my eyes. I believe they would have kept me there all day had not Madame appeared on the scene. The sight of her triple chin and heavy moustache quickly restored order and I was at length allowed to purchase an elegant silk handkerchief edged with the beautiful lacework for which Ypres has for centuries been famous.

At four o'clock in the afternoon came a noise like an express train and a shell from a big howitzer fell in the middle of the market place. Pandemonium! People scattered in all directions. They would have done well to have cleared out of the ill-fated town altogether. Nobody knew it at the time but the destruction of Ypres had begun. Within a week the whole town was a mass of deserted ruins. Those houses which escaped demolition by the shells were gutted by the fire which raged incessantly day and night. Not one remained untouched.

I have often thought since of that first shell that fell in Ypres. The inhabitants were so unprepared for what was to follow. Yet they must have often realised they were living, as it were, under the shadow of a volcano. It was not that the place had never been shelled before. They had already seen their Cloth Hall and their Cathedral reduced to ruins.

I suppose a very similar situation existed in Herculaneum or Pompeii before they were wiped out through a different agency. When the first lava began to flow and the first cinders to rain, I can imagine they shrugged their shoulders and said " C'est la guerre ! " or whatever

c*   73

their native equivalent for blaming it on to the volcano might be.

Not that I have very much right to criticise. We four were sitting in a café when it happened and, at the time, thought it a huge joke. Perhaps I may blame our hilarity on to Ernest. Parisian that he was, he had, by discreet enquiry, discovered that the proprietor possessed a stock of Pernod. After that he would not rest until the cork was drawn. At first taste I thought the stuff worse than the potato cognac. After the second glass, however, I began to like it. It certainly was the most potent liquor I have ever sampled. It went to the head as only absinthe can.

I well remember a French soldier who expressed a desire to learn how the English rifle worked. I was only too ready to oblige him.

" Like this ! " I cried and pointing the muzzle at the café window to where the sky showed blue above the square, I pulled the trigger.

Thanks to Ernest's French we got out through the back way just as the military police were entering at the front. Mine host was too upset and excited to remember to charge me for the glass of his front window. He only wanted to see me go. We went back to the battalion after that.

Ten days later we marched up to Ypres and took over from the Royal Horse Guards Blue. They formed part of the First Cavalry Division who were holding the salient as dismounted cavalry. Our billets were under the ramparts, in huge semicircular cellars.

What a change had come over the town since my first visit. Instead of throngs of people the streets were deserted. Pleasant cafés and inviting shops were now heaps of rubble. Here and there lay scattered belongings, evidence of the hasty flight of their owners.

Tommy Atkins does not miss much that may be for his benefit. Even before we arrived some of the troops had discovered that the gallant townsmen, unable to carry away their stocks of wine, had buried it carefully in their gardens.

Trenches were never dug with greater will than went to the unearthing of the spoil. Unfortunately the authorities, spoil sports, quickly stepped in and confined all troops to their quarters. Tantalus never looked at his grapes with greater longing than that with which we looked out over the city. Wine of every description to be had for the taking. Enough for everybody. Too much, in fact. Hence the guard which kept us in our cellars.

Restrictions were made to be circumvented. I approached Captain Boyle, and after making out a case that the troops would die of boredom unless a concert was immediately organised, I pointed out that the town must be full of unused pianos, and got permission to go out and look for one. I selected five strong men and the rest was easy.

We tried about a hundred houses before we found a piano that was undamaged. Then we dug one out from under some debris in a convent. A handcart provided the necessary transport and we started on the return journey. We duly reached the ramparts, but although a score of willing hands came forward to help us with our load, we strenuously refused any assistance. Carefully we lowered our precious burden on to the floor of the cellar. Then the reason for our zeal was exposed. The frame of the instrument was filled chock full with bottles of wine.

We went up to the trenches that same night, rather unexpectedly. I am very much afraid that some members of C Company were looking on the War through rosier-coloured spectacles than the Ypres Salient warranted.

The following is an extract from a letter I wrote home on the 8th June :

" . . . We are in a very interesting part of the line, and I am looking forward to some fun in the sniping line. We are going to these trenches for the first time to-night. I hear that in one place there is a château in the hands of the Huns whilst we hold the stable thereof. Rather a deadlock. What! I think we certainly shall have some fun there. The only trouble is that as we have been four days in reserve, we have eaten most of our extras, and consequently we shall have to live on rations almost entirely in the trench. . . . "

The Ypres Salient was undoubtedly the most interesting part of the line in 1915. Time and again the Hun had broken through, only to be hurled back by a counter-attack to his previous position. There were no supports nearer than the ramparts at Ypres. Just the front line boldly jutting out into the enemy territory.

I have never been able to determine why we continued to hold it from a practical point of view. On the face of things it would seem that it would have been good strategy to withdraw. But, from the angle of *moral,* its tenure was invaluable to us. Every time the Hun failed to capture the Salient his troops were reminded of the invincibility of British Infantry. Every time we succeeded in driving the enemy back our troops were cheered with the knowledge that superior numbers did not necessarily mean superior fighting capability. I can imagine General Smith-Dorrien chewing his iron grey moustache and bristling with pride at the thought of what the Salient meant to Britain. It stood as a monument of our indomitable resolution never to recognise defeat.

All the same it was a pretty warm spot for those who had to occupy it. Its shape and size made it vulnerable from all quarters. The Hun could shell the trench with equal facility either from the back or front. So much so that one never knew whether the shells passing overhead were one's own or the enemy's.

At the very pinnacle of the Salient stood Hooge. Stood is merely a figure of speech unless one takes it in the past tense, for, even when we first saw it, not one brick rested on another. I had expected to see the shell of the original château but it simply did not exist. Neither did the stables. It was true that Fritz occupied the site of the château whilst we occupied the site of the stables. The distance between them was about fifteen yards. Both sides remained on the qui vive day and night although both refrained from offensive measures. No one knew what sort of upheaval might not arise from a carelessly fired rifle.

My Company was further away to the left. Here the trenches were between one hundred and fifty and two hundred yards apart and the situation was less tense. However, there was no more roaming No Man's Land at night. Even Captain Boyle went no further than to examine our barbed wire entanglements.

We spent three days in the front line without any unusual incidents and then marched back eight miles for a rest. I was already beginning to distrust the word rest. It usually meant that we spent our time on fatigues and worked considerably harder than we ever had to in the front line, or else we got nicely settled and then had to uproot ourselves and march to another part of the line. This time it was neither. Instead, we had scarcely reached our destination when a rumour ran through the battalion that we were going back almost immediately to take part in an attack.

At last ! I was as excited as a girl going to her first dance. But even then I was not satisfied. We were not to make the charge but were to go over in support behind the first line. I was terribly disappointed. All the fun would be over before we reached the enemy position. At least so I thought in my ignorance. For this was not going to be a small affair like the Moulin Rouge. This was a full-dress parade of the whole of the

Third Division. We were going to push the end out of the Salient. We might finish up anywhere. The fighting Third. Haldane's cast-iron Division. We were irresistible. The enemy would be swept away like grass before the scythe. And we were only in the second line. I could have wept with chagrin.

It was very interesting to see how everybody reacted to the news. Some were very glum and went about with long faces as if the end of the world was at hand. Others took the attitude that it would be a distinct change from the monotony of trench life. A few frankly funked it, but on the whole I think we were a fairly hearty Company.

Captain Boyle metaphorically ground his teeth. It was the best bit of news he had heard since he first came out. His only regret was that he was not physically strong enough to carry a rifle and bayonet. Percy maintained his usual attitude of stoical calm but expressed a fervent hope that the Hun trenches we were going to capture would be cleaner and less smelly than our usual ones.

I was a little worried about Ernest. He had a presentiment that he was going to be killed and nothing I could say would alter his conviction. He even went so far as to write home and say good-bye to his father, so firm was his conviction. The possibility did not in the least affect his great natural courage. His only fear was lest he should be wiped out in the initial advance before he had a chance to take two or three of the enemy with him.

I myself had no morbid thoughts. I simply looked upon the coming adventure much in the same way that I looked forward to an exciting game of Rugger before the War. I wanted to distinguish myself and I was determined to seize on any chance that came my way. I also wanted to christen my bayonet, although I did not see much chance of that in the second line. Roll on the hours until we move off. Let us get at them !

CHAPTER EIGHT

I CHARGE!

THE 15th June, 1915, was a broiling hot summer's day. There was scarcely a breath of wind as we set off on the eight mile march which would take us to our " jumping off " position. The Poperinghe-Ypres road was, as usual, crowded with traffic ; troops in large and small parties, some in full equipment, some in light fatigue dress ; limbers drawn by horses, limbers drawn by mules ; endless ammunition columns ; siege guns and howitzers ; strings of lorries ; motor cycle despatch riders ; every conceivable branch of the Service was represented going about its business in orderly confusion. Even the cavalry, who, since the inception of trench warfare were rather out of fashion, had their part in the pageant. They sat their horses with the same erectness as in peace time, but their drab equipment was in sad contrast to the shining breast-plates, scarlet cloaks, and nodding plumes with which they entrance the nursemaids in the Mall.

On this occasion they rode with something of an air. When we succeeded in boring a hole through the enemy's defences on the following morning they would come once more into their own. Thundering hoofs and steaming nostrils would race in pursuit of a flying enemy. Sharp steel and quivering lance would clear the way for us to consolidate our victory.

We did not go right into Ypres. We turned off short of Hell Fire Corner across the fields. In one of these **a** stray shell knocked the Adjutant off his horse, though luckily without killing him. It was only a minor incident but it warned us that we were under fire ; our big adventure had commenced.

A student of psychology would notice a subtle difference between troops marching away from the line for a rest, and the same troops going up the line into action. Leaving the line, when every step means a further distance from bullets and shells, there is an atmosphere of gaiety ; songs are heard, jokes are exchanged, laughter is frequent. Going up, on the other hand, is a very different business. There is an air of seriousness, remarks are answered in monosyllables ; men are mostly silent, occupied with their own thoughts. Some laugh and chatter from a sense of bravado, or to prevent their imaginations from becoming too active ; others to bolster up the shrinking spirits of their weaker comrades. Only a few are natural.

On this occasion there was a tenseness in the bearing of the battalion quite different from our normal visits to the trenches. We started off with a swing as if we were going for a route march. Everyone walked jauntily and one could sense the excitement in the air. Gradually this spirit faded, helped no doubt by the heat of the day and the sweat of marching. The wounding of the Adjutant was like the period at the end of a paragraph. After that first shell scarcely a word was spoken. We were going into something of which we had no experience. No man felt sure he would live through the coming ordeal.

We were halted in a field to await the coming of dusk. Tea was provided from the cookers which were afterwards taken back to the transport field. I wonder how many watched them go off with envious eyes for the Company cooks and the drivers. I wonder whether any of those returning envied us.

We moved forward in the twilight in single file. Our

way lay along a railway line and we stumbled forward and cursed the sleepers. They were either too far apart or too near ; I have never been able to determine which. What I am sure of is that they are damnably awkward things to walk on, especially in full battle order.

At last we reached our position. It consisted of row after row of narrow shallow trenches, each row being intended to accommodate successive waves of attacking troops. We were herded into ours literally like sardines. There was no room to lie down ; the trench was too narrow to sit down in except sideways ; if one stood up, one was head and shoulders over the top. Such were the quarters in which we were to pass the night.

Ernest and I and Percy got to work with our entrenching tools and hollowed out a space so that we could crouch in some sort of comfort. It was not worth while to put in too much work as we should only be there for a few hours. As it was it took us over an hour to get ourselves settled.

Smoking was strictly forbidden in case Fritz spotted the glow of the cigarettes, but of course we smoked. We managed to get a light from an apparatus which I had had sent out from home. It consisted of some sort of cord which was ignited by sparking a flint with a small wheel. Its merit lay in the fact that it glowed without making a flame. We were able to light up in perfect safety.

Sleep was out of the question. Not only was I too uncomfortable but I was far too excited. In a few hours I was to go over the top for the first time. I felt no trace of fear or even nervousness ; only an anxiety to get started. The hours seemed interminable. Would the dawn never come ?

Fritz started spasmodic shelling in the small hours. Whether he suspected anything or not I cannot say. I do not think he can have done for a concentrated bombardment of these congested assembly trenches would have meant a massacre. The stuff he was sending over was shrapnel and he caused some casualties, although not in our trench.

About an hour before zero hour a message came down the line that I was to report to Captain Boyle. Thankfully I climbed out of my cramped lodgement and made my way to Company Headquarters. Captain Boyle had great news for me. Two men were required to accompany the first wave as a connecting link. I was one of the two chosen ; the other was a fellow called Springfield, whose father was editor of *London Opinion*.

Springy and I were delighted. I especially so. My ambition was to be realised. I was to take part in a real charge. With luck I might bayonet a Hun.

We reported to Captain Spooner of the 1st Lincolns. The Lincolns were in the British front-line trench and were consequently very much more comfortable than we were in the assembly trenches. We had scarcely arrived when the barrage commenced.

Bang ! Bang ! Bang ! Bang ! Bang ! Swish, swish, swish, swish. Crump ! Crump ! Crump ! Crump ! Crump ! Deafening pandemonium ! One had to shout in one's neighbour's ear to make oneself heard at all. I knew the Hun was replying because an occasional shower of dust and earth descended on my head, but the continuous noise of guns and shells rendered my sense of hearing completely inoperative. Guns firing and shells bursting were so intermingled, friend and foe, that there was one endless succession of shattering detonations.

Springy and I stood and waited ; Captain Spooner from time to time looked at his watch ; the men of the Lincolns fidgeted with their equipment. My pulse raced ; the blood pounded through my veins. I looked at Springy and grinned ; Springy grinned back. Only a few more minutes.

At last Captain Spooner turned and smiled. His lips

formed the words, " Only a minute to go ! " Instantly all was bustle and confusion. Short three-rung ladders were placed against the parapet. A man stood by each one, his foot on the first step, his rifle and bayonet swung over his shoulder.

Captain Spooner raised his hand ; then swarmed up the ladder in front of him. I followed close at his heels. Springy was only a second behind me. Right and left along the line men were clambering over the top.

With the memory of the Moulin Rouge fresh in my mind, I fully expected that we should be met by a withering fire as we emerged into the open. I anticipated the crackle of machine-guns, the rattle of musketry, the sweeping away of our gallant charge. Except that I never once dreamed or considered that I myself should be hit. Even in this first attack I had the extraordinary feeling of being myself exempt, though not to the same degree as later on when I was an officer. I shall therefore leave the analysis of this peculiar sense until I record the period when it became more pronounced.

Instead of a hail of machine-gun and rifle bullets, there was—nothing ! Not a sign of life was to be seen anywhere around the enemy position. Overhead the shells still whined and screeched ; behind us and in front great spouts of earth went up in bursts. The noise was deafening, but from the menacing line of earth works opposite, not so much as a puff of smoke.

Just ahead of me Captain Spooner ran in a steady jog-trot across No Man's Land. Right and left stretched long lines of troops. All were running forward, their rifles gripped in their hands.

Four hundred yards to go ! We ran steadily on. Springy and I had lengthened our stride until we were right at Captain Spooner's heels. Still not a movement in the trench we were rapidly approaching.

What should we meet when we got there, I wondered ?

Perhaps they were reserving their fire until the last moment. Perhaps a hidden machine-gun nest would suddenly sweep us away like chaff before the wind. Or it might be that the infantry would rise to meet us with a yell in a counter bayonet charge. I clenched my teeth and gripped my rifle tighter.

Ten yards from the trench Springy and I both sprinted. Two minds with but a single thought. We both wanted to be first to engage the enemy. There was no wire to bother us. It had been utterly destroyed by our fierce barrage. We passed Captain Spooner in a flash.

What a shock met my eyes as I mounted the German parapet. The trench was full of men ; men with sightless eyes and waxen faces. Each gripped his rifle and leaned against the side of the trench in an attitude of defence, but all were dead. We were attacking a position held by corpses !

For a single moment I could not believe my eyes. I thought it must be some trick of the Hun to fill the trench with dummies, the better to lure us into a trap. Then, when at length I realised what I was looking at, I felt suddenly sick with horror. This was unvarnished war ; war with the gloves off. There was something ludicrous about that trench of dead men. One wanted to laugh at their comical appearance. There was also something fine ; every man in his place with his face towards the enemy. But mostly they aroused a feeling of pity. Death must have come to them so suddenly, without giving them a chance in their own defence. They certainly gave me a very different reception from anything I had anticipated.

The Lincolns swept past and on to the second line. Springy and I turned and ran back to the " jumping off " trench. Our job was to report that the first German line was clear. Captain Boyle was standing on the parapet talking to Major Ward. I informed them that the Lincolns had gone on, and then, without waiting for the battalion to advance, ran back again to the German position. I suppose, strictly speaking, I should have rejoined my section. But I had received no definite orders to do so and I wanted to get back to the Lincolns and see some of the fighting. I was still sure there would be a hand to hand contest.

There was now considerably more activity from the Huns. Machine-guns were intermingling their clatter with the roar of the shells. They were firing from some reserve positions, and I could hear the whine and whistle of the bullets as they passed me or ricochetted overhead.

The German trench I had first entered was situated on the edge of a small wood. This I now passed through to the second trench at the back; then on up to the German communication trench. Here I saw my first live Hun. He was lying half in and half out of a dug-out, pinned down by a beam of wood which prevented him from moving the lower part of his body. All the same he was full of fight. He had a thin face with an aquiline nose on which were perched steel-rimmed glasses. He reminded me forcibly of a German master we had at my preparatory school. In his hand he held an automatic with which he was taking pot-shots at whoever passed him. He had killed one man and wounded one, and I arrived just in time to see a Tommy stick him with his bayonet.

I passed right up the communication trench until I found the Lincolns. They were holding what had been the fourth German line which they were putting in a condition of defence. I made the mistake of reporting to Captain Spooner who at once ordered me to rejoin my unit. There was no sign of any hand-to-hand fighting anywhere up there. All was peace and quiet. The Hun had cleared out without waiting for the British advance. I concluded the whole thing was over and returned to the wood.

Corpses were lying all over the place, British and German. In the third German line I came across a dead Fusilier armed with an axe. The edge was red with blood. He had reverted to the weapon of his forefathers.

For the dead I could do nothing, but there were also plenty of wounded. These I attempted to tie up with their field-dressings. Several were able to walk and I showed them the way back to the British position. One man I shall always remember. He was hit in one of the arteries just above the heart and the blood was pumping out in regular beats. He was a big Highlander with a gigantic chest and only his great physique prevented him from collapsing. I plugged his wound as well as I could, but I have often wondered since whether he survived. The pity of it !

At one place a Hun had fallen and jammed the communication trench with his body. I took him by the shoulders and another fellow by the feet with the intention of heaving him out of the way. We lifted him all right, but a shell had taken away the top of his head which fell forward and poured the whole of his brains over my tunic. I was red from chin to ankle. From my appearance I might have been in the bloodiest of bloody encounters. And yet my bayonet was virgin steel ; not one single round had been fired through my rifle.

I was beginning to think it was about time I found my own battalion when I encountered Captain Holliday, battalion machine-gun officer, bringing up the two battalion machine-guns. He was short-handed and at once gave me orders that I was to attach myself to his unit. There was nothing for it but to obey and, for the rest of that day, I became a machine-gunner.

Captain Holliday selected a position in the second German line on the edge of the wood with a field of fire of some eighteen hundred yards. The guns were soon erected and we sat down to await eventualities. We were not long in idleness. Almost immediately the Hun started a counter-attack against the position slightly to our left. We could see the lines of field grey advancing and our guns got in some effective bursts of fire. I was supernumerary to the gun teams and amused myself with my rifle, though I cannot say definitely whether I succeeded in hitting anybody. Eventually the attack failed largely owing to the effectiveness of the shrapnel from our field-guns.

Up to this point the German artillery had been fairly quiet. They had probably been waiting to determine the relative positions of their own and our troops. But now they commenced a bombardment which was to last the whole of that day. Every gun they could bring to bear was turned on the captured position. Shells were coming from the front, from the sides and, owing to our being at the top of the Salient, from the back. Field-guns, six-inch howitzers, eight-inch howitzers, four point nines, nine point twos, every calibre of armament that they possessed poured a continual stream of lead into our position. We had made a fairly easy capture ; we were to be made to pay for our subsequent tenure.

For some reason which I have never been able to determine the spot where our two machine-guns were situated was never touched. We did not have a single casuality all day. A tiny oasis in a desert of desolation. I do not think there was a single other part of the wood that escaped.

I had plenty of opportunity to see all that was happening. Captain Holliday employed me all day long as a runner. I carried messages to all four of our Company Headquarters, and even back to the old British position. The whole time I was running the gauntlet of the rain of shells. Everywhere I went I heard tales of the continually mounting list of our casualties. Colonel Treffry was hit in the head in the first advance. Major Ward was hit. Captain Boyle was hit. "Duggie" Davis was hit. Laurie MacArthur was hit. I began to wonder whether we should have any battalion left at all. It was the same with the men. Name after name was reported killed and wounded. Unfortunately I could get no news of those in my own platoon. They had gone forward to the fourth German line and nothing was known of them. I could only hope that my particular friends were as lucky as I was myself.

We had found a wounded officer in the Lincolns in front of our trench when we first arrived. There was no stretcher available to get him away, so we made him as comfortable as possible in a shell-hole behind our position. He was hit in the stomach, and although he cried out all day for water it would have been the utmost folly to have given him any. I went out and sat with him in the intervals when I was unemployed. He did not know of my presence, but I felt I was doing everything possible for him.

The day slowly passed in a tornado of the worst shelling I was ever in during the whole War. Towards five o'clock Fritz made another counter-attack and we were able to let off some of our feelings towards him in the form of rifle and machine-gun fire. Any pity I had felt for any of them in the earlier part of the day was swallowed up in an intense hatred against them for what they were doing to my comrades in arms. Everywhere I went I found maimed and shattered bodies, many of them of men with whom I had been laughing and joking on the previous day. My regiment was being subjected to the most searching test that any troops can undergo—the test of steadiness under shell-fire when there is no question of retreat and no chance of retaliation. Throughout the day they stuck to their posts and did everything that the Staff asked of them. Had the enemy counter-attacks been more vigorous they would have repelled them. They were undoubtedly one of the most steadfast units in the Division.

Night came at last and with it a slight diminution in the shelling. On one of my message-carrying errands I returned with welcome news. We were to be relieved by fresh troops.

It was two o'clock in the morning before we heard the welcome jingle of accoutrements. Followed a hail in broad Scotch. The Gordons were arriving to take our place.

We waited until the Gordons had fixed their machine-guns in position and had got some idea of the lie of the land in front, and then set off on our journey of retirement. Back through the wood of death ; gas still hung about the trees. Back across No Man's Land that was. Back to the Menin Road. I led the way as I was most familiar with the country. My rifle was slung over my shoulder and in each hand I carried a box of machine-gun ammunition.

The machine-gun limber was waiting just outside the Menin Gate at Ypres. We piled on the guns and equipment as quickly as possible for the Hun artillery was searching the road with shrapnel. We had completed our task and were in the act of moving off when a big white woolly bear burst dead overhead. The bullets sprayed the road all round us and in front. By a miracle no one was touched. The horses reared in fright and set off at a gallop. We followed at a fast trot. Under the arch of the Menin Gate we paused and got our breath. Then passed through into the comparative safety of the city. Our first attack was over.

CHAPTER NINE

I BECOME A BOMBER

IN the light of experience gained later in the War the attack on the 16th June, 1915, was a hopeless failure. Units did not understand their objectives and either overran them or failed to reach them at all. There was little or no attempt at consolidation. The Artillery were unable to give their support when it was most needed because they had no idea where our troops were located. Soldiers of different units were too hopelessly mixed to be properly commanded. There was a needless loss of life through overcrowding.

No doubt the Staff learnt a great deal from the mistakes made. They certainly had some first-class evidence from the Brigade Major of the Seventh Brigade. He was here, there and everywhere all day long, doing his best to evolve order out of chaos. He was magnificent. Without his personal example and guidance the whole of the attacking force might easily have been hurled back in a rout to where it started.

As it was we took and held two lines of trenches. That was the sum total of our achievement. What we set out to do I have no idea. We certainly did not do it. The cavalry were never brought forward; there was no use for them as we had not broken through. The affair resulted in a gesture.

But even if the Staff learnt nothing, I learnt a lot. Not that my knowledge came to me all in a flash. Far from it. But, later on, when I had command of men myself, I remembered the lesson of my first attack and profited by it.

One thing was obvious from the first. We mustered in the transport field the following day a bare three hundred and fifty men all told. Our battalion of the finest material that the Country could ever have for officers had been thrown away uselessly to provide the Hun artillery with a target. Later on when those men were badly needed for the new armies it was remembered that they were under the turf of Flanders.

Percy was amongst those who survived ; Ernest was missing. Percy, the collar of his tunic torn away by a bit of flying shrapnel, told me how it happened. The platoon had gone forward to the fourth German line. In one of the counter-attacks they had been forced to retire. Ernest was left behind, a bullet through his thigh. We heard in due course that he died in a German hospital some ten days later, but I like to imagine that he fired his rifle right up to the moment they took him. His premonition nearly came true. I missed him terribly ; he had the heart of a lion. His memory is perpetuated with me in his razor strop which I still use daily. I wanted one of his effects for remembrance sake and the strop was the only thing I felt I could conveniently carry.

Very few of our officers came through and the command of the battalion temporarily devolved on the " Pull-through " until a fresh commanding officer could arrive from England. C Company was taken over by " Bun " Morphy, a command he was to hold with one brief interval throughout the rest of the campaign. Bun was always one of the most popular men in the Regiment. He is an Irishman with a fund of dry humour all his own ; never at a loss for a word or a quick ripost of repartee. He carried his name through the War with the magnificent record of always doing thoroughly the job that lay nearest.

91

I was promoted full corporal. Without exception I think the position of full corporal the nicest rank in the Army. Certainly it is in Wartime. On fatigues, for instance, the party is either large enough to need a sergeant in charge or small enough for a lance-corporal. The full corporal misses it both ways.

Despite our heavy losses we were only given a few days' breathing space before we went back to the line again. It was very interesting to see the position we had held under such arduous conditions in daylight without the storm of shells that rendered full appreciation of the locality impossible. The wood was now reduced to a collection of stumps of trees but the trenches were very good. Considerable work had been put into them in the form of sandbag revetments and new barbed-wire entanglements had been erected in front.

We learnt on our arrival that a night attack was to be delivered somewhere on our right the following night by the 1st Wilts. A hundred of us were required to take over and hold the trench after it was captured. According to the map there would be one ticklish spot where a barricade would have to be made in the German communication trench, forming a sap-head running out in front of our new position. I at once volunteered myself and my section for the job. I wanted an opportunity to avenge Ernest whose real fate we did not then know.

Night time in a wood is always an eerie business. Trees stirred by the wind make ghostly whisperings and sounds seemed muffled and unreal. As usual we moved into position hours before the time the show was to commence. With the knowledge of what we had experienced a few days before, we did not doubt that we should have a pretty sticky time. My section especially would be in a position of utmost danger. Yet I felt no fear; only a hope that this time I might have a chance to kill some Huns at close quarters.

Captain Holliday was in charge of our detachment. He came along the line to see how we were and asked me if I would like some bombs. Now up to that time I had never even seen a bomb, but I eagerly agreed. I accompanied him back to Headquarters and was given a sort of waistcoat which I tied on in front of me and a dozen bombs of the type called Mark 6 and 7, light and heavy. One ignited a sort of glorified match by striking it against a brassard like the enlarged side of a matchbox tied on the arm. The match lit a fuse which would burn for five seconds. Having got the fuse under way one threw the bomb into the enemy trench where it either exploded or else it did not. Added to my normal equipment I found the outfit damned heavy and uncomfortable.

When I arrived back to where my section waited they looked at me askance. I think they thought I was as likely to blow them up as the Hun. Fortunately possibly for all parties I did not have to use my newly acquired weapon. For some reason the attack was called off at the last minute and I was not put to the test.

I mention the incident because it was the very first occasion on which I handled a bomb. Afterwards I handled thousands of every type and description. But I really think that it was the way I was introduced to them which first fired my imagination. The bomb is essentially a close-quarter weapon. I was hoping to get to close quarters. Night time in a wood; the moon showing through the trees, her peaceful radiance in strong contrast to the errand on which we were engaged. The loss of Ernest fresh in my mind. My spirit all worked up with the determination to kill or be killed. These were all contributory factors which decided me later on to become a bomber.

We did sixteen days in the trenches that trip, alternating between the front line and reserve. When we eventually returned to our transport field for a rest we found a new draft waiting for us which brought our numbers up again.

I have often wondered whether rest is the right word to use in connection with the short periods we spent out of the line in the summer of 1915. We would march in to the transport field which was situated about eight miles behind the Salient and form up by companies. Then we would pile arms in four long lines. The order would be given to dismiss and there we were. The accommodation provided for our shelter was the sky above and the earth beneath. If the sky was clouded and the earth soaking it did not make any difference. True we were allowed the use of our overcoats out of the line and one blanket apiece. But as often as not they were saturated when we got them. Even so it was better than when we were actually in the trenches. There we had no overcoats at all. If it rained we got wet and that was all there was to it.

I wrote a very illuminating letter home on the 23rd July.

MY DEAREST MATER,

Thanks very much for your letter and for sending off the parcel which has not yet arrived. I am not unfortunately coming home to-day, but I hope to next week unless something unforeseen occurs. Anyhow, mine is the next name on the leave list. Our three weeks' rest only got as far as nine days and now we find ourselves back in the trenches again so you see nothing in my present life is at all certain. We came up at a day's notice. On the seventh day we moved our bivouac to another field and as we thought we should be there for a fortnight we got some hop-poles and made ourselves a jolly decent shelter with our wetter-sheets for the roof and sacking for the walls and dug a shallow trench all round to drain the rain away. It took us nearly a whole day. Two days after we had to pull the whole lot down again, fill in the trench, and march off. Rotten luck! What?

We are now in a wood in dug-outs in reserve, and we go into the actual trenches to-morrow for nine days. With any luck I shall leave them before then to come home so you will get me straight from the trenches. Some sensation, though I hope to clean myself up before I ring the bell at Tidbury somewhere about seven in the morning. Incidentally I have not washed for a fortnight as the only water near us was in a duck-weedy pond with a dead dog in it and I don't want skin disease. Mrs. B. sent Percy out some excellent lice powder with which I managed to kill all my menagerie. I think it is strong enough to kill elephants. Anyhow it got into a cut and gave me a slight blood poisoning in the leg; not enough to prevent me going into the village a mile away for some grub, but sufficient excuse for me (old soldier) not to attend any of the silly parades and route marches with which we were pestered during our so-called rest. You see I got my name on the sick list by parading before the doctor every day for some rotten ointment which I did not use as it only irritated the part. I used boracic. It is quite gone now.

Percy also paraded only on a few occasions so we had a lot of time together. I am glad to say he is much better, probably because we have not seen anything but rain lately. Still I think the root of the matter is that his heart is not strong enough to stand the strain of this arduous life. Though I hope you won't think my tales of the life are a fraud when you see the excellent condition I am in.

Percy had to go on a fatigue last night carrying some heavy stuff about three miles to some trenches some way from here and of course the paths are thick

with clay after the rain. He arrived back at 2 a.m.
absolutely whacked. I really don't think he will stick
it much longer though he has the spirit of a lion. Of
course it rained all the time and we have no overcoats
here so the poor devils were soaked through besides
being covered with mud where they had fallen into
shell-holes or on the extremely slippery ground. Our
dug-out lets water like a sieve and I woke up at eight
this morning to find I had spent the night in a pool of
water. At present it has no effect on me, though this
sleeping in water and continually getting soaked through
will probably mean chronic rheumatism in a few years.
Still no matter.

I nearly got a soft job the other day without knowing
it. I was told to parade before the Commanding
Officer, and of course I went, not knowing
of any misdeed. He asked me a few questions,
and I afterwards heard that it was a job as Brigade
bomb-instructor to assist one of our officers in a school
of bombing. The Brigade apparently did not want it
after all and so the job fell through. But I have been
appointed corporal in charge of our Company bombers,
sixteen men. Percy would be one so I had to let him.
So now, in the event of us attacking or being attacked,
we chuck bombs. I shall be in a position to turn
anarchist after the War. Anyhow, I know a good bit
about bombs and grenades. They are very jolly things
to play with. Would you like one as a souvenir ?

By the way, I enclose that picture I forgot before.

Bye bye now.

I received my leave warrant on the 31st July.

CHAPTER TEN

LEAVE

THERE were six of us in the batch in which I went on leave. Four sergeants, a private in the Signallers and me. We took the train at Poperinghe and were duly deposited at Victoria Station at five o'clock the next morning. Sergeant Edmund Sharpe lived at Croydon; I at Wallington. We hired a taxi and drove down together, stopping once on the way at a coffee stall for some coffee and cakes.

My home was not astir when I arrived so I took a stone and flung it up at my sister's bedroom window. In my excitement I chose rather a large stone and it smashed a pane of glass. What did I care? I was home on leave after ten and a half months at the front.

They were all very pleased to see me, especially my mother. She never said a word about the anxiety she had been through. All she wanted to ensure was that I had the best possible time whilst I was home. She is undoubtedly the best mother in the world.

My first action after breakfast was to visit the family of Her whom I adored. She herself had joined the staff of a hospital in London, but her two sisters were at home; the next best thing. I was always very fond of both of them. They had kept me well supplied with letters and parcels. Now I was home they went out of their way to make my leave a great success. I do not know whether they knew at this time of my great attachment to their sister. They must have guessed that I was keen, but no one but myself could know how my keenness had grown into an obsession in the still night watches.

I phoned the hospital and arranged to meet her on the following day. Her two sisters, my sister, she and I lunched together at the Piccadilly Hotel. Afterwards we drove round and round Regent's Park in a taxi. It was not perhaps a very romantic way of spending the afternoon, but My Lady had to return to hospital and there was no time to do anything more exciting.

I was thrilled. To feel her sitting next to me ; to hear her speak ; to know that I was with her. Regent's Park was Heaven and the taxi a golden chariot.

I knew I loved her then. I would have done any-thing in the world she asked me. I was a knight fighting for her protection. I was a door-mat for her feet. If she wished me to go alone across No Man's Land in broad daylight I would have done it. She held my heart in the hollow of her hand.

She knew, of course. She was a woman and her instinct told her. Not one syllable did I breathe that all the world might not have heard. Yet she knew that she had only to hold up one finger and I was hers.

Four and a half days' leave ! Theatres, lunches, dinners, shops, presents for everybody. I shocked my Yorkshire father by my extravagance. But I knew, what he had no means of appreciating, that I might be enjoying myself in London for the last time. Eat, drink and be merry for to-morrow may bring a bullet or a shell ! That was my motto and I lived right up to it. I don't think I had more than three hours' sleep a day the whole time I was home.

Our return train left Victoria at five o'clock in the afternoon. There was a terrific crowd on the platform, mothers, sweethearts, wives. Our six managed to secure a compartment to ourselves. My father arrived just before the train moved off. He had a parcel under his arm which he thrust through the carriage window. It contained two bottles of whisky and two of brandy. A welcome stirrup-cup !

We finished one bottle of each by the time we reached Folkestone. Who can blame us ? We were returning to the jaws of death after a brief interlude of life.

The signaller johnnie got a bit tight and had to be assisted on to the boat. I rather think he had been saying good-bye all the afternoon. The rest of us were merely happy.

My eldest sister met us at Boulogne. She was acting as the Matron of a French hospital and was wearing her uniform. She had ordered a meal for us at the Hotel de Louvre where the sight of her French uniform worked wonders. Nothing was too good for us. Madame herself showed us to a table in the centre of the room. She said to my sister : " You are looking after the French *soldats blessés*, I will look after your English soldiers." The room was filled with officers of all ranks, both Staff and regimental. They got scant attention until our needs were satisfied. From the glowering looks that were thrown in our direction I do not think we were at all popular. Fortunately we had taken the precaution to park the signaller in the railway carriage which was to take us back to Pop. The rest of us boarded the train as it was on the move.

The following day we found the familiar transport field in the same old spot. The battalion was in the line and we went up that night and joined them. In my pack I carried an unopened bottle of whisky and an unopened bottle of brandy. They were for my section and great was the rejoicing when I produced them.

I retired by myself and sat down with my thoughts. My leave was over. I had enjoyed every minute of it but I was not sorry to be back. I should not have cared to remain in England knowing that the Regiment was in the line. I should have felt a shirker.

Something had happened to me whilst I was home and I had to get my new bearings. I knew now what I wanted; for the first time in my life I began to think of marriage. Of course she was ever so much too good for me. I recognised that from the start. She was the most divine, glorious creature that ever breathed. Try how I would, I knew I could never reach her standard. But I must do my best. She could never be expected to fall in love with a common soldier; one of the herd. But supposing I got a commission? Supposing I went to her as an officer covered in decorations? Then perhaps she might deign to smile on me.

She herself had suggested a commission. She had even laughed at me because I had not already applied for one. Not that I believed she really cared one way or the other at that time. I think she just looked on me as a good friend who deserved the greater comfort of an officer's life. Perhaps she was feminine enough to prefer to be seen in London with an escort in an officer's tunic rather than a corporal's. Who knows? Anyway, her words, lightly uttered, bore fruit. Ambition was born within me. I would apply for a commission. I would also take every chance that came my way to earn distinction. Her knight would win his spurs.

The following day I filled in my application form.

CHAPTER ELEVEN

MY FIRST COMMAND

THE trenches we were occupying were at St. Julien, to the left of the Salient. The battalion was in reserve which meant a fairly cushy time. Apart from fatigues and carrying parties we had very little to do. The time passed pleasantly enough with plenty of bridge and vingt-et-un.

Owing to the nature of the soil in the Salient it was impossible to dig trenches. Any excavations below two feet were instantly filled with water. Consequently all the trenches in this part of the line consisted of barricades made of sandbags. Millions and millions and millions of sandbags all laboriously filled by hand. Trenches constructed in this way had the advantage of being cleaner to live in than ditches dug in the soil, but they also had the disadvantage that they stuck up above the ground and offered a bigger target to enemy artillery.

At one point at St. Julien our trench ran across the road which was generally used by troops going to and from the front line. One of our duties was to supply a guard on this road post. It consisted of a corporal or lance-corporal and three men. There was no particular reason for a guard at this spot, except that we had to have a certain number of sentries on duty and a gap in our line seemed to be the obvious place for one group of them.

In due course it fell to my lot to be in charge of this

road post. My tour of duty happened to coincide with a startling rumour that an enemy spy had been going and coming through our lines dressed in British uniform. There was a short notice about it in orders, warning everybody to be on the look out for a man believed to be about six foot in height and of a swarthy complexion.

I was full of excitement. With the desire to distinguish myself hot within me, I made sure my opportunity had arrived. To capture an enemy spy red-handed ! What a big step along the path to make my lady proud of me !

Of course he would pass through the road post on the very night I was on duty. In common decency he could not do anything else. The problem remained how was I to recognise him ? How was I to pick him out from the hundreds of men in British uniform who would be passing and re-passing all night long ? It was going to be a difficult business. Still there was one clue which would enable me to limit my search. The man had to be six feet.

At once an idea occurred to me. With the assistance of my guard, whom I had succeeded in firing with my own enthusiasm, I stretched a cord across the road at exactly six feet from the ground. In the darkness it would be invisible. Everyone who passed under it could go on his way without question ; those who touched it we would hold for closer investigation.

Our trap set we waited eagerly for our quarry to walk into it. String after string of men filed past ; none of whom could possibly be suspect. Several times the cord was touched or dragged down by some tommy's rifle. Much bad language was used on both sides. Midnight came and went. We were still spyless.

Two o'clock in the morning and the zeal of my guard was fast evaporating. I was as keen as ever. He must come. Suddenly rapid footsteps were heard approaching from the direction of the front line trench. One man by himself. I hissed a whispered word of warning and clutched my rifle firmly.

A man came quickly through the gap in the barricade. A tall man whose face showed swarthy in the moonlight. He wore a small black moustache and had about him an air of command such as one might expect in a Prussian officer. The cord caught his cap and sent it flying. With a muttered oath he turned to pick it up.

" Hands up ! " roared the sentry on duty.

The man turned quickly, his hands above his head. Nobody presumed to ignore such an order in the Salient in '15 when fingers were light on the trigger.

" Friend," he stated genially. " Company quarter-master-sergeant, 3rd Worcesters."

I ignored his explanation and ran my hands quickly over his body for the hidden weapon. There was none.

" What's the meaning of this blankety nonsense ? " enquired the C.Q.M.S. warmly.

" I'm sorry, quartermaster-sergeant," I said quietly, " I'm not satisfied as to your identity."

" You're not satisfied ? " he thundered. " What the hell d'you mean ? Tell that man to put up his rifle. I'm in a hurry."

The geniality had changed to wrath. But the more he blustered, the more determined I became. I was sure now that I had got the right man.

" You keep quite still," I advised him. " Unless of course you want a bullet through you. You'll have to stay here until you've been seen by an officer."

I instructed one of my men to go along and rouse Captain Morphy. My suspect grew livid with rage.

" Don't be such a bloody fool ! " he shouted. " I'm catching the leave train to-night and I'm late as it is."

" I can't help that," I remarked imperturbably. " You shouldn't be walking about up here by yourself ; then you wouldn't be held up."

103

We waited some half-hour. Captain Morphy was asleep between blankets and was none too pleased to be disturbed. Whilst we waited I was subjected to the most blood-curdling barrage of bad language that a regular C.Q.M.S. could concoct. My ancestors, my personal characteristics, my future destination, as were outlined in a wealth of vivid imprecations. Hearing him I grew more and more convinced that I had made a mistake. No Hun could have such a mastery of the hidden lights of the English language. When Captain Morphy arrived he confirmed my impression and the unfortunate quarter-bloke was allowed to go on his way. I sincerely hope he caught his leave train. I had undoubtedly distinguished myself, but I did not write and tell My Lady about it.

We completed twelve days in the trenches at St. Julien and after the usual four days' rest moved back to the scene of our attack in June. The trenches we had formerly occupied were an absolute shambles, half-full of unburied corpses killed in some action that had taken place meanwhile. We moved in to a new trench dug just behind the old position. Even here all digging operation ɪencountered bodies.

With the knowledge that I would soon be an officer, I spent as much time as possible roaming round No Man's Land. The Huns were now eight hundred yards away and there was plenty to see in the intervening space. On one of these excursions I came across an excellent Burberry with only five small shrapnel holes in it and which I promptly annexed. By it, in the bottom of the shell-hole where I found it, was a solitary head. It stood upright in the centre of the crater and there was no trace of the body to which it belonged anywhere near it. For some reason it fascinated me. It looked so droll and yet so pathetic. To whom had it belonged ? Was he friend or foe ? Had death overtaken him whilst he was dashing forward in a charge full of the lust of battle or had he been cowering down in sickening fear, his nerve shattered by the thunder of bursting shells ? I hoped he was a fighter who had gone down with his face to the enemy, his courage high and his mouth set in grim determination. That was how I hoped to die if I had to ; though I should have liked one second's warning so that I could breathe Her name. Afterwards, if my head remained to mark the spot, I should like it to be pointing to the trenches I had never reached.

We had a listening outpost in the middle of this desolation. It was three hundred yards in front of our line. I was thoroughly happy the night I was in charge of it. I had twelve men under me and we were entirely cut off from everybody. My first independent command. My attitude is best revealed by an extract from a letter I wrote home on the 29th August whilst actually in the outpost.

" —We ought to have a lively time on this outpost with corpses all round us. It is in a ditch with practically no protection of any sort from the inclemency of the weather. Still, I shall take jolly good care that if the Huns try to surprise us none of my command will have their tails down and the surprisers will be surprised. I have about a hundred bombs with me so ought to make a good show. Talking of bombs, bombers in an attack now carry a mace which consists of a stout handle with a huge lump of iron on the end. One, found on the late battlefield, had a number of large spikes in the end as well. It shows what modern warfare is coming to when we have to go back to the dark ages for our weapons. They will be serving out bows and poisoned arrows next——"

Fritz remained quiet so I was not put to the test. Perhaps it was as well because I should never have retired and we should merely have been wiped out. As it was we completed sixteen days in the line and then went back for the usual four days' rest.

I did not return to the line with the battalion. Instead I was sent to the Second Army Grenade School at Terdeghen to learn all about bombs. Terdeghen is situated at the foot of Cassel Hill and it was very quiet and peaceful there after the Ypres Salient. The weather was perfect and I thoroughly enjoyed myself apart from the course which interested me intensely.

My Lady's birthday fell in September and of course I wrote to commemorate it. My pen ran away with me, and I went on to tell her that I hoped she would become my wife as soon as the War was over. I rounded off with a simple declaration of my abject devotion.

The course lasted a fortnight during which time I acquired a complete knowledge of every bomb and grenade in use by either ourselves or the Hun at that time. They also taught me a method of trench-clearing for a bombing party about which I shall have a good deal to relate later on. For the moment I will content myself with a short description of how the party was made up.

It consisted of eight men. Two ordinary riflemen with bayonets fixed led the way. Their job was to protect the bomb-throwers from surprise and tackle any of the enemy they came across. Behind them came the first bomb-thrower followed by a man carrying a supply of bombs for him to throw. Then came another bomb-thrower and another carrier. Then the leader of the party and lastly a spare man who acted as an extra carrier or could be used to replace casualties according to circumstances.

The order was entirely wrong as I definitely proved on two separate occasions. I shall explain in due course where it was wrong and how I reshuffled it under the stress of action. In the meantime I should like to record that the Second Army Grenade Course was a very fine one. Without the knowledge I gained there I doubt very much whether I should be alive to-day.

The battalion was in the line when I returned. I

reported first of all to the transport field where I found everyone in the deepest gloom. A tragedy of the first magnitude had occurred. Four of our officers had been killed by a shell which landed in their dug-out from behind. Amongst them was the officer in charge of the newly-formed bombing platoon which had been got together whilst I was away.

I reported my return to Battalion Headquarters on my way up to the line that night and was informed, to my astonishment, that I was to take charge of the bombing platoon. The Commanding Officer went on to say that an attack was to be made on the 25th September, and that I was to construct fourteen bomb shelters, proof against shell-fire for reserve supplies of bombs for the attacking troops. A herculean task, but what a chance to show what I was made of !

The chief difficulty lay in the fact that Fritz was subjecting the whole position to an intensive bombardment at irregular intervals throughout the day and night. No one knew when one of these strafes might occur. The moment one commenced the whole of the troops in the front line were withdrawn into the communication and support trenches so as to minimise the number of casualties. That is to say, the whole of the troops with the exception of the bombing platoon. A subtle difference.

The bombing platoon was scattered in threes and fours over the whole of the battalion front. Some were in small sap-heads ; others were in listening posts. There were thirty-two of them in all, eight from each Company. None of them had more than the most elementary knowledge of bombs. Yet all were great-hearted soldiers imbued with the right fighting spirit. With the knowledge that the safety of the front line depended on them, they would all have died cheerfully at their posts rather than yield a foot. Truly a command of which I shall always be proud.

I used to go round and visit them all at intervals. It took me about two hours to get from one end of the line to the other. It would have taken twenty minutes to have walked without stopping. The whole trench system was an intricate maze of winding lanes. At one point there was an enormous mine-crater. It was in the side of this that the dug-out was situated where our four officers were killed. It was an eerie place to pass through at night. If ever the stage was set for the ghosts of the thousands of dead killed in the Salient, here was a natural amphitheatre.

I think Fritz must have guessed he was to be attacked ; he was so infernally jumpy. Every few hours the whole of his artillery would start up and, concentrating on the area round Hooge where we hung on by our teeth, give the whole position a thorough drenching. It was one of the hottest spots I was in during the whole War.

It was manifestly impossible for the bombing platoon to attempt the construction of the fourteen bomb shelters. I realised that from the first. Besides, it was in no way a specialist job. I went down to Headquarters and had a chat with the Colonel. I returned to the line with a *carte blanche* order addressed to all officers commanding Companies that I was to be given as many men as I required. The rest was easy. With adequate labour the shelters were constructed under my supervision. All the work had to be done at night. Fritz never gave us sufficiently long intervals of quiet in the daytime.

At last all was in readiness. On the night of the twenty-fourth we were relieved by the troops who were going to make the attack. I led my command from the trenches. We halted when we were clear of the reserve line for the customary ten minutes' rest. Every man jack of us fell asleep. We were dead tired with the strain we had undergone. I myself had been five days and nights in the line without once closing my eyes.

I was promoted a sergeant the following day. Later I received a card from the Divisional General in acknowledgement of the work I put in.

I append a copy of it below :

THIRD DIVISION
BRITISH EXPEDITIONARY FORCE

1023 Corporal A. O. Pollard,

Hon. Artillery Company.

Your Commanding Officer and Brigade Commander have informed me that you distinguished yourself in the field.

I have read their report with much pleasure.

A. Haldane, *Major-General.*

Commanding 3rd Division.

CHAPTER TWELVE

A BOMBING ATTACK

THE reply to my proposal of marriage reached me on the morning of the twenty-ninth, and my castle of dreams came tumbling about my ears. She expressed herself as amazed that such an idea could ever have entered my head. Because she had sent me letters and chocolates and cigarettes I had absolutely no right to assume that she had any more regard for me than she had for any other soldier serving his country at the front. It was merely that I was a friend of the family and one of the few men she knew personally in France. She wound up with the statement that if she ever married, which was improbable, I should certainly be about the last man whose proposal she would entertain.

That was that. My romance had reached an abrupt termination. She was right, dead right. In fact, I never knew her to be anything else. Her logic was invariably unassailable. I had no right to assume that she might care for me. I was a sentimental, romantic, love-lorn fool whilst she was a clear-thinking, consistent, materialist who considered things as they were and not as they might be.

It hit me damned hard, though. I had been so optimistic about her coming to care for me. Not that I presumed to imagine that she would reply to my letter saying that she already loved me or anything like that. But I thought that she might have given me a tiny ray of hope. She might have let me down rather more gently. She could have suggested that I was rather young to think about marriage and had I not better leave the subject until the War was over or something like that. As it was she plunged me right into the depths.

I went down the village that night and attempted to bury my sorrows under a pile of empty champagne bottles. Fortunately I was far too physically fit to get tight. I was merely a trifle muddled when I returned to camp. Sufficiently to trip over the guy ropes of my tent and that sort of thing. For some reason unknown the authorities had supplied us with a proper camp. We were not destined to stay in it very long.

At one o'clock in the morning I became conscious that someone was shaking me roughly.

" What the hell do you want ? " I muttered sleepily. " Why can't you let me alone ? "

" Stand to ! " bellowed an urgent voice. " Stand to, man ! We've orders to move off at once ! "

The words gradually penetrated my consciousness and I aroused myself with a jerk. I stretched out my hands for my boots. A moment later I was out in the open getting on with my job.

There was no time to stop and ask questions. Orders had been issued and they must be obeyed. As platoon sergeant of the bombers I had my hands full. Every man had to receive his day's rations ; blankets had to be rolled up and returned to the stores ; tents had to be tidied ; there were a hundred and one things to organise and arrange.

We had spent the five days since we came down from the crater in practising the bombers in trench-clearing and the various other exercises I had learnt at the school. I had been hard at it all day lecturing on bombs and generally training my platoon. All our practice material had to be accounted for to the Quartermaster.

At last we were ready. I fell the men in and reported to Second Lieutenant E. W. Hammond, who had been newly appointed to command the bombing platoon. We stood easy whilst the rest of the battalion were forming up. I breathed a sigh of relief that my little lot were not the last. Then my heart suddenly went into my mouth. With a terrible feeling of nakedness I realised that I had omitted to put on my puttees.

I rushed back to my tent, but they were nowhere to be found. To this day I have no idea what became of them. I searched high and low but in vain. There was nothing for it but to parade without them.

Unfortunately for me the bombing platoon marched at the head of the battalion. This meant that Mr. Hammond and I followed immediately behind the Colonel and the Adjutant. I was all right so long as darkness lasted, but of course the Colonel spotted me at the first halt after dawn. He called me up and gave me a terrific strafing about my dignity as a freshly appointed sergeant. I ought to set an example to the men instead of which I had dared to appear on parade without my puttees, etc. etc. I said I was very sorry but I simply could not find them, and that was all there was to it. The Colonel eventually turned away. He was very displeased.

Nine miles to the top of the Salient. We halted just outside the commencement of the communication trench for breakfast. Bully beef and biscuits washed down by a hot gripe made me feel my normal cheery self. The Colonel and Adjutant went off to Brigade Headquarters for a conference. We waited patiently wondering what was the meaning of our nocturnal disturbance.

After some while a messenger arrived to fetch Mr. Hammond. Rumour was already rife that we were going into action and I began to get excited. Was I so soon to have a chance to blood my new bombing platoon ? I was.

Hammy returned about the middle of the morning full of the tremendous news. Fritz had blown a mine under the fourth battalion of the Middlesex in the middle of the night, killing ninety men. In the subsequent scrap they had succeeded in occupying the mine-crater. We were to counter-attack and turn them out. Only the bombing platoon would be employed. The rest of the battalion would be in reserve.

I mentally rubbed my hands. These were great tidings. It was the biggest opportunity I had had in the whole War to show what I could do. My bombers that I had trained would cover themselves with glory. The position was as good as taken.

I had not the slightest fear or thought that I might be hit. Only an overwhelming feeling of thankfulness that we had been chosen for the task. At once I set about last minute instructions to the men, detailing them to their tasks, reminding them of what they had been taught, firing them to do their best with my own enthusiasm.

The attack was timed for three o'clock in the afternoon. There was to be a short artillery barrage and then we were to advance. The platoon was divided into two parts. Hammy was to take one half whilst I took the other. We were to work round the sides of the crater until we met.

We got into our respective positions a little after two. Up to that time I had been too busy making preparations to think of anything else. Now I had a little leisure and my thoughts turned naturally to the letter which burned in my pocket. Even if I did put up a good show it would not make any difference now. She would be interested—as a friend. No longer could I consider myself as a knight fighting for his lady. I was merely a soldier doing a routine job for his country.

All the same I was determined to do my best. Fighting was in my blood and I was looking forward eagerly to the moment when we should begin. I was resolved to reach the other side of the crater before Hammy. To me the whole affair was a game to be entered into in a spirit of competition.

At ten minutes to three five bombers turned up from the Royal Scots. They were all privates without a leader, and they were rather in a muddle as to what they were supposed to do. I learnt afterwards that they were intended to make the attack whilst I supported them. Whoever framed that order did not know the sort of fellow I was. Nobody was going to take the glory of that scrap from me.

None of the five had a hat. They explained that it was believed that some of the Huns might be dressed in Royal Scots uniforms, and that their regiment had received instructions not to wear their hats to distinguish them from possible enemies. Personally I think it was all tommy rot. The Huns would have run too great a risk of being killed by their own people to have attempted such a stunt.

It was rather interesting to think of the Royal Scots fighting side by side with the Honourable Artillery Company. They are the oldest regiment of regulars in the British Army, being significantly nicknamed Pontius Pilate's Bodyguard. We are actually the oldest British Regiment. We received our Charter of Incorporation in the year 1537. History takes our formation back a good many years before that. We are supposed to have sprung from a company of archers banded together in the reign of William Rufus for the protection of the City of London. Sir Arthur Conan Doyle's *The White Company* was probably written round a legend of the Regiment.

Punctually at three o'clock the barrage opened. It was only a travesty of the barrage of the sixteenth of June. Shouted commands could be heard easily.

At once we moved forward in the correct formation

of a trench clearing party as laid down by the Second Army Grenade School. Our way lay down the old communication trench. Fifty yards from where we started the trench was blocked with a barricade which brought the leading bayonet man up short. I gave the word to start bombing. The first bomb thrower pulled the safety pin out of the bomb he was holding, swung his arm, a long throw—a pause—bang! The fray had commenced.

The mine crater was situated in the middle of a wood —Sanctuary Wood, Hooge. Tall trees were all about us, their green foliage making a strange setting for our savage sport. The bombs burst with a curious hollow sound, the explosion deadened by the tree trunks.

Bang! Bang! Bang! Zunk! Zunk! Zunk! The bombers were now getting down to it with a will. The worthy Royal Scots were joining in and throwing as fast as they could pick up their bombs and pull the safety pins.

For three minutes or so we had it all our own way. Then a shout from one of the men warned me that retaliation had commenced. A thing like a jam tin on the end of a stick came hurtling through the air ; landed on our parapet ; a moment whilst it lay hissing— crack! Instantly it was followed by another. Then another and another. Fritz could give as good as he received.

This was all very well, but as long as we were confronted by that barricade progress was impossible. The affair was degenerating into a sort of snowball match except that the snowballs were deadly missiles. I must get either through or round that barricade. But, first of all, I had to deal with a grave danger that had arisen amongst my own rank and file.

The bombs in use in those days were of many and varied types. They were also of two classes—percussion and time. The time bombs were exploded by a five-second fuse which was generally considered to give the thrower a sufficient margin of safety to set it off and throw it, and for it to reach its destination before it burst. The percussion bombs, as the name implies, exploded on impact. They were mounted on a short stick at the end of which were a number of tapes or streamers which spread out in the air to ensure that the weapon landed on its head, which was essential to ensure detonation. If the thrower inadvertently banged the head against the side of the trench whilst stretching back his arm to throw it, it would immediately explode to his undoing.

That was the danger to which my party was exposed. Neither my own men nor the Royal Scots knew a great deal about bombing. There were a number of these stick grenades in the trench, and they were handling them as carelessly as though they were as innocuous as playthings. Every instant I expected to see one blow up in our midst.

There was only one thing to be done. I took all the stick bombs and threw them in a heap over the parapet. Then gave instructions that no one was to use another of them if he should come across one. We had plenty of time bombs. Thus one danger was averted and at the same time I learnt a lesson. Stick bombs cannot be safely handled by troops in the excitement of action.

Now for the barricade. At once I learned my second lesson. In the order of advance laid down at the Grenade School, the leader of the party occupied fifth place. I wonder whether the man who instigated that order ever tried to urge five men to cross a seven-foot barricade in the teeth of the enemy before he tried himself. I very much doubt it. My experience throughout the War was that you could lead men anywhere provided you yourself were prepared to go first and show them the way. I went first round that barricade.

Before I made the attempt I ordered the spare men to collect piles of bombs in readiness. Three throwers were to drop five bombs each over the barricade in quick succession and then concentrate on throwing as far beyond it as possible.

Immediately my miniature barrage commenced I climbed out of the trench closely followed by half a dozen men. We were at once exposed to enfilading rifle fire from the Hun lines. I lost four men out of my six getting round that barricade, but I got round. Two dead Huns were lying in the trench, victims of my bomb attack. As I jumped down off the parapet I nearly joined them. A Hun bomb exploded right in front of me, hurling me back against the barricade from which I sank in a heap on the ground. My senses reeled, and I believe that for a moment I was unconscious.

" Are you done in, sergeant ? "

The urgency of the tones of one of my two followers who had successfully run the gauntlet of the barricade brought me to myself. I sat up and shook myself like a dog. All over my body were little prickles where splinters of the bomb had pierced my flesh.

" I'm all right," I cried. " Get on up to the next traverse and keep guard ! "

We had driven Fritz back a little way and I wanted to renew contact with him whilst he was on the run. The two men kept guard whilst I called over the barricade for reinforcements. With the help of the rest of the party we pulled down the sandbags until they were only waist high so that more of my men could join us. Almost immediately we had renewed our attack.

But now Fritz was employing another device to hold us up. Unable to stop us with his bombers he had posted a number of snipers in the branches of the trees. From a distance of forty yards they were pouring shot after shot into my party with deadly accuracy. Casualties were coming much too fast for my liking. Still never a man shirked, either of our Regiment or the Royal Scots. All were head up and heart up in the fight.

I began to experience that curious sense of detachment to which I have alluded before. It was just as though my spirit was detached from my body. My physical body became a machine doing the bidding, coolly and accurately, which my spirit dictated. Something outside myself seemed to tell me what to do, so that I was never at a loss. At the same time I felt quite certain that I should pull through.

There was one curious incident which I shall never forget. I was giving orders to one of the Royal Scots. He was a little man of not more than five feet four inches. He was standing in front of me listening to what I had to say, when—whist!—a bullet took him through the throat and he fell dead at my feet. Now, I am six feet two and was as much exposed to the enemy as he was. Ever since I have asked myself what caused the Hun sniper to select the little Scot for a target instead of me. The knowledge that some fate had spared me on that occasion helped me considerably in the later years of the War. I used to think, if not once, why not twice ? Well, after all, it was so. Otherwise I should not be writing this account now.

There were plenty of chances to get hit in that scrap. We started with sixteen of our men and five Royal Scots. Only seven came out unscathed. I was not amongst them.

We made better progress after we passed the barricade. Fritz did not like our hail of bombs and retreated steadily before us. Presently we came to a second barricade, though not such a high one as the first. I think this must have been part of the original British front line. Anyway, I was more than half way round the side of the crater, although I could neither see nor hear signs of Hammy's half of the platoon.

My blood was now thoroughly up. I was determined to take that crater or bust. We dealt with that barricade exactly the same as we had done the first. This time without any casualties. Bombs were running short and I sent back a messenger for further supplies. I hopped back on our side of the barricade to fetch a sack of bombs which was lying there. I picked them up and was in the act of handing them to a man who had turned to take them from me when he suddenly pitched forward on his face. At the same time my right arm fell to my side and the sack of bombs dropped to the ground.

I tried to lift my arm again but could not move it. That's damned funny, I thought. What's wrong with it ? I had felt absolutely nothing. I was still wondering why I could not move it when my knees suddenly gave way beneath me. Trees merged with sky ; the sand-bagged sides of the trench tilted, then began slowly to revolve. The trees and the sky joined in the kaleidoscope. Hell ! I thought, I'm going to faint. I mustn't do that. Only girls faint.

Someone held a water-bottle to my lips and I sipped gratefully. It was rum and water, the nectar of the gods. I looked down at my silly useless arm. The shoulder of my tunic was stained crimson, the stain was slowly spreading.

I got to my feet and leaned against the parapet. This was too annoying just as we had got them on the run. I did not mind so much about my arm if only my legs would regain their strength. I could still direct operations with one arm.

" I'll have to rest a bit, you chaps. Get back behind this barricade and hold on there until I recover. I'll be all right in a minute."

I sank slowly back to the ground. The thunder of

shells, the zip of bullets, the vicious cracking of bombs faded from my consciousness. The fight in Sanctuary Wood was over as far as I was concerned. For the first time in my life I discovered that fainting is not confined solely to the gentler sex.

BOOK TWO

FULFILMENT

CHAPTER ONE

BLIGHTY

SERGEANT A. O. POLLARD, of the Honourable Artillery Company, has been awarded the Distinguished Conduct Medal, for "conspicuous gallantry on September 30 at Sanctuary Wood during the bombing fight. Although severely wounded, Sergeant Pollard continued to throw bombs, at the same time issuing orders to and encouraging his men. By his example and gallant conduct he renewed confidence amongst the bombers at a time when they were shaken, owing to the enemy being in superior numbers and throwing many more bombs than were available on our side. He did not give up until he fell, severely wounded for the second time."

Such was the official account of my efforts in the counter-attack which appeared in the *London Gazette* in due course.

Two days later I received a letter from my Commanding Officer.

I have great pleasure in handing you the enclosed card from the G.O.C. 3rd Division in acknowledgment of certain of your services prior to the 30th September. I was very pleased to learn that for your distinguished services on that date you received the D.C.M., but at the same time it was a matter of sincere regret to me, and still is, that you were not awarded the higher recognition for which I strongly recommended you, and which I think you well earned.

Trusting that you are making good progress and that you will soon be fit and well again,

Yours sincerely,

HAROLD T. HANSON, LT.-COL.,

Commdg. 1/II.A.C.

The card referred to is the one set out on page 109.

He had recommended me for the Victoria Cross. I was delighted but at the same time amazed to think I had done anything worthy of a decoration at all. Eye-witnesses of the affair apparently thought otherwise.

The news reached me whilst I was lying in hospital at Crumpsall Infirmary, Manchester, whither the Hospital authorities had carried me. My wounds were more troublesome than serious. The effect of the bomb had been merely to leave a number of very small splinters distributed over my body. These would work themselves out in due course and required no treatment. The bullet wound in my shoulder was another matter.

The sniper who had fired the shot had aimed at the man on the other side of the barricade to whom I was handing the sack of bombs. From a distance of forty yards the velocity of the bullet had been sufficient to carry it right through the body of the man it had killed and into my shoulder. But it must have turned over in the short interval between us as it hit me base first. Had it struck me with the point leading it would probably have gone right through and smashed my shoulder blade. As it was it came to rest deeply imbedded in the fleshy part of my shoulder, having missed nearly everything of importance. It had cut a minor artery which caused the loss of blood from which I fainted. It also flicked the median nerve which supplies the first and second fingers of the hand.

I was able to walk down to the dressing station with the help of one of my men. Here I was roughly dressed and was injected with an antitoxin against tetanus. There was no time for more as the doctor was inundated with wound cases of all descriptions. They were mostly the result of Hun counter shell-fire directed against the battalion which was supporting our attack.

They wanted to send me down on a stretcher, but there were so many stretcher cases already that I volunteered to walk. The ambulance could only get to a spot about a mile away. I nearly reached it. There were only a few more yards to go when I fainted again. When I came round I was in the Casualty Clearing Station.

The following day I was evacuated to the base. The C.C.S never kept anybody longer than twenty-four hours if they could help it. They had to be always ready for a fresh influx.

One of the R.A.M.C. orderlies was extremely attentive to me. He went out of his way to make me as comfortable as possible. At the time I was very grateful. Later, when I reached the base, I changed my mind.

The base hospital was staffed by nurses. As soon as I was tucked into bed my nurse asked me if I would like her to get me some cigarettes. Of course I eagerly agreed, but when she went through my effects to find some money to pay for them, there was none to be found. My R.A.M.C. orderly friend had reimbursed himself for the trouble he took to the extent of some ninety francs. Rob All My Comrades.

Even when one is lying helplessly wounded there is nothing so trying as to be entirely without money. One has a feeling of inferiority. Nurse came to the rescue and volunteered to fetch an officer from my Regiment who was in the same hospital. A few minutes later I was delighted to see Hammy.

His half of the bombing platoon had fared even worse than mine. The sniping had been deadly and they were nearly wiped out. Hammy himself had been hit quite early on. It was only a slight flesh wound in the arm, just sufficient to take him home. He lent me £5, which completely restored my self-sufficiency.

I had my first operation whilst I was in the Base Hospital. They thought the bullet might be lying somewhere near the surface; in any case they wanted to arrange a channel to drain the suppuration. They failed to find the bullet and I was duly marked for Blighty.

The hospital ship landed its convoy at Dover where we were transferred to the train. I was naturally hoping that we were making for London, but to my bitter disappointment we did not stop until we reached Manchester.

It was my first visit to the North of England and I found the people very kind and hospitable. I was the only non-commissioned officer in a ward of nineteen men and, by virtue of my rank, was accorded special privileges. After a second operation in which the bullet was found and extracted, I was allowed to do pretty much as I liked. I could, for instance, go down into the City, which I did nearly every day.

There was plenty to do. All the theatres were free to wounded soldiers which was a great boon. But my favourite haunt was the Midland Hotel where I used to go for tea. It was all great fun and a very definite change from the rigorous life at the front.

Of course my people came up North to see me and I had the pleasure of my mother staying in Manchester for several days. I think she was overjoyed to have me home wounded. She was assured of my safety for a time at any rate.

Actually I should have been just as safe had I remained with the battalion. Immediately after the affair in Sanctuary Wood they were withdrawn from the line altogether. They went back to St. Omer where they were turned into an Officers' Training Corps. Their place in the Division was taken by the Artists' Rifles who had not, so far, had a taste of the front line at all.

The knowledge relieved my mind considerably. I should have hated to be confined to hospital in England knowing that the Boys were wearily toiling up the Poperinghe-Ypres Road for a periodical sojourn in the line. And it would have been positive torture had they gone into action without me.

I had plenty of time for thought whilst I was in Crumpsall Infirmary, and I took the opportunity to considerably straighten out my ideas on things. Up to now I had merely been a boy playing with realities. The rebuff to my proposal of marriage; the experience of my wound; but mostly the knowledge that I could successfully lead men in action had turned me into a man. I had had my preparation. I knew what responsibility entailed. Now I must shape my course for the future.

What was I fighting for ? That was the first question to be decided. Like thousands of other men of my own age I had enlisted at the outbreak of war to fight for my Country. Why had we been sent out to the front to risk our lives whilst others, as physically fit as ourselves, stayed at home in soft jobs. The simplest way of answering this question is to say that some had to go and some had to remain behind. Those who went, went because they wanted to go. Those who stayed behind either had businesses which required their presence, wives who would be penniless if they fell, or else they lacked the inclination.

It seems to me that the principle on which we recruited the huge army for the defence of our Empire was fundamentally wrong. Where the safety of the Nation is at stake it should not be left to the individual taste of each citizen to decide whether or not he will take part in protecting his own property and dependents. It is a National affair and should be treated as such. Otherwise the greatest burden may fall on the wrong people.

To carry the point to an absurdity, supposing no one had volunteered for active service in 1914. The elected rulers of the country had declared war in the National interest and the campaign would have been left to a handful of Regulars and Territorials. The result would have been an early defeat and the British Empire would have crashed to the ground.

Some people might contend that that would be a small matter compared with what they might choose to term the liberty of the individual. They would argue, why should a man go to war against his will? My reply is that if, when his country is threatened by another Power, he is not prepared to defend it, then he has no right to any of the benefits which his Country normally provides. The protection of the police ; the comfort of the roads ; the benefit of the dole ; any law of any sort or description ; he should fend for himself, his hand against every man, every man's hand against him. He has no place in the general community.

After all what is a Nation or an Empire except a banding together of individuals in a common interest ? Such a banding together is a fundamental instinct of life. It is found even amongst herds of animals. The cattle on the plains keep together in a bunch, the females, the young and the old steers in the middle with the young prime bulls on the outside. The same system pertains and has pertained throughout the ages in all forms of tribal life. The young fit men protect the women, the children and the old men. Refusal on the part of a warrior to do his duty meant certain ignominy and probable death. The law of the tribe was based on self-preservation.

Had our National leaders based their arrangements on this fundamental principle the War, as far as the British Empire was concerned, would have been conducted in a far more efficient manner with the result that it would have been decided sooner and, what is more important, would have cost considerably less both in lives and money.

I am not going to suggest that the country should have been organised on these lines so early as 1914. I do not think that anybody, with the exception of Lord Kitchener and perhaps a few others, foresaw the duration of the struggle to which we had committed ourselves. But, as soon as it was realised that a deadlock had been reached on the Western front, steps should have been taken to organise the Country on business lines, allotting each and every man to the job for which he was best suited. Taken on a big scale it would have been comparatively easy.

The first step would have been to pass an Act of Parliament proclaiming a National Emergency and ordering every individual who was a British subject to hold himself or herself in readiness to take up any work that might be allotted. It would be impossible to absorb everyone immediately and people would have followed the ordinary routine of their lives until they were needed.

For the actual conduct of the War two classes of troops were required—attackers and defenders. Experience has proved that men between eighteen and twenty-five make the best attacking troops, whilst those from twenty-five to thirty make the best defenders. The reason is not very far to seek, the young men have the dash whilst the older ones have the caution. Men over thirty would have been used on the lines of communication or in the making of munitions as required and according to their individual abilities. Women would have been organised along similar lines. And everybody would have received rations from the common store and equal pay.

There were incidents during the War when munition workers went on strike for increased pay. I am sorry for them in that their mentality must have been of a very low order or they could never have done such a thing. Not only did they let down their brothers who were fighting in their interests but they jeopardised their own safety, a thing the lowest types of savages would have scorned to do. They have my pity in that they did not know what they were doing.

The strikers were persuaded to resume work by the leaders appointed by the majority of the Nation giving them what they asked. Whoever the men were who were responsible for such a measure, and however much they argue that they achieved their immediate object, the fact remains that they recklessly expended money with which they had been entrusted by the Country as a whole, in satisfying the greed of some of its least worthy citizens. Acclamations that munitions were supplied when they were most needed covered up the ominous facts that the shortage of shells and the treacherous attitude of the munition workers were directly due to the lack of organisation and foresight on the part of those who were entrusted by the electors with the conduct of the State.

I did not of course reach all these conclusions whilst I was laid up in Manchester. They are the result of a very deep study of the War and its management. But I did get as far as realising that it is the duty of every man, woman, and child to serve the State before himself or herself. By doing so each individual is carrying out that essential principle of life laid down by Jesus Christ, " Do unto others as you would that they should do to you."

I had fought for a year for the joy of it, for My Lady, because I happened to be sent to France, for no particular reason. In future I would fight for my Country because it was the right thing to do. Such was my state of mind when I was discharged from hospital with my wound cured.

To my inexpressible horror I discovered that I was marked permanently unfit for further active service.

CHAPTER TWO

HOME SERVICE

I SUPPOSE that many men in my position would have been satisfied with the hospital verdict. They would have felt that they had done everything possible to satisfy their personal honour, as well as their duty to their Country. In the idiom of the period they would have " done their bit."

My make-up is admittedly a peculiar one. The thought that I was condemned to stay at home whilst my beloved Regiment was on active service was intolerable. For the time being they were fortunately out of the line. I would lie low and get my strength back. But the moment I heard a whisper that they might be returning to the line, I was determined to join them by hook or by crook.

I left the hospital at the end of November. They gave me a fortnight's leave which I spent at home. One of my first acts after reaching London was to ring up My Lady at her hospital and ask her to meet me.

Our rendezvous was at Cannon Street Station and I can see her now as she came towards me. She wore a purple costume with a small, close-fitting hat of the same colour. Her face was framed in black fox furs, and a wisp of golden hair which peeped coquettishly over one ear wound itself tightly round my heart.

A wave of inexpressible longing swept over me as I stepped forward to greet her. To me she was so utterly desirable. In the year I had spent in Flanders I had endowed her with every womanly virtue. In my fancy no woman ever lived who could compare with her. Surely she would withdraw the letter she had written me and give me some hope that she might some day come to care.

My belief was short-lived. We had tea together in a quiet restaurant. She went straight to the point and told me definitely, once and for all, that she would never marry me. She even went so far as to declare that she would never even see me again unless I gave her my word of honour that I would never refer to the question of our engagement. I might know her as a friend but nothing more.

Of course I promised. I was incapable of putting her out of my life. I would have accepted any conditions so long as I might see her occasionally and be with her. I smiled as I gave my word ; a smile that hid a breaking heart.

At the end of my fortnight's leave I reported to the reserve battalion of my Regiment. They were lying in billets at Richmond and I was greeted by a number of familiar faces. Captain Boyle was almost the first person I saw. He told me he was very proud of me which meant considerably more to me than the greater effusion of lesser men.

Colonel Evans, commanding the battalion, a tall, fine-looking man with a long white moustache, also greeted me warmly. He referred to the fact that I had put in my papers for a commission and offered me one in the Regiment. No reward could have given me greater pleasure. It was a higher honour than I had ever contemplated. I accepted enthusiastically.

I also paid a visit to the doctor. He was lying on his back on a camp-bed when I visited his sanctum, a big powerfully built man with a strong face and a humorous twinkle in his eye. He wanted to look at my wound. When I showed it to him he remarked that it was very inflamed and that the scar looked as though it was stretched. I explained that I had attempted to practice bomb-throwing in the garden; a remark that caused him a lot of amusement. He told me I had better have another fortnight's sick leave which carried me over Christmas.

When I did eventually join the battalion for duty there were only a few days before my commission came through. It was dated the 19th January, 1916, and I was one of the proudest men in the world.

It was an extraordinarily happy mess that I was privileged to join. It is a rule in our Regiment that every officer must serve in the ranks. The result was that quite half the people I encountered had been privates with me in France. Even so I might have felt a trifle awkward in my new surroundings had it not been for Hammy. He took me in hand and guided me past all the pit-falls which might have tripped me.

I did not do ordinary Company duty but, by virtue of my experience, was attached to the battalion bombing school. This was in charge of Captain " Ted " Ellis, and he was assisted by Hammy and Geoffrey Withers.

Almost immediately I was sent on a three weeks' training course for Officers at Chelsea Barracks. When I rejoined the battalion they had moved to quarters at Blackheath.

Here we built an enormous pit where the troops could practise throwing live bombs. It was situated in the grounds of " The Cedars," a big mansion that had been taken over for the men's billets. We had the greatest fun slinging over grenades every day, getting potential bombers used to handling the real thing.

My life at Blackheath was a merry one. As often as we could get leave three or four of us used to go up to town for the evening. With our youth and high spirits we became involved in many exciting adventures.

I remember one night Hammy and Geoff Withers and I dined together at the Trocadero. We were just leaving when we ran into Tubby Ayres, a fellow from one of our batteries, home on leave, dining with his father and uncle. They insisted that we should join them at a show. Father Ayres was the host and selected a review called *Snowballs* at the Pavilion. We occupied seats in the third row of the stalls and settled down to watch. All went well until the last scene when all the chorus came on and pelted the audience with snowballs made of wool. We three bombers replied heartily and fierce was the battle that raged. Immediately in front of me sat a fat man in a dinner jacket who was enjoying himself immensely. In searching for ammunition I came across his opera hat and coat neatly arranged under his chair. The discovery was too much for me and a second later the opera hat was sailing towards the stage. One of the chorus caught it and put it on amidst roars of applause.

Nobody laughed more heartily than the fat man until suddenly something familiar about the hat caught his eye. His face wore a slightly stricken look as he searched vainly under the seat. Then he turned to me.

" Did you throw my hat on the stage ? " he demanded.

" Certainly," I smiled.

He beckoned an attendant who was standing in the gangway. I took the opportunity to send his coat after his hat. The attendant was most rude.

" Wotcher mean by interfering with this gentleman's clothes ? " he enquired truculently.

" I mean this," I explained and standing up I removed his cap and flung it after the other things.

He was furious but as he did not like to tackle me by himself, retired for assistance. We decided that the moment had arrived to beat it.

The story of my life at Blackheath would not be complete did I not take the opportunity to introduce Captain Charles Osmond. Ossy went out with the first battalion as transport officer but was soon employed on

Company duty. He is a little man, about five feet four in height and has the distinction of being one of the only two Britishers who ever won the black belt of Japan for jiu-jitsu. He is one of the most popular men I have ever encountered ; in fact I have never heard any one speak of him except with the highest regard and praise. I have always looked up to him as a wise counsellor and friend.

He was wounded on the 16th June during the attack. At home he was second-in-command of the Company that Captain Boyle was commanding. Of course I had met him a good many times in France but then he was an officer and I was in the ranks and things were naturally different. At Blackheath I could talk to him as man to man and I found him extraordinarily interesting. He could converse on practically every subject under the sun and used to tell stories that held me spellbound.

There were many others I would like to write about had I the space. Monty, Skipper Ellis, Noel Simmons, Percy Finch, Teddie Garrard, " Duggie " Davis whose servant I had been, these and many more all had a part in my life. All were of the best type of Britisher and carried out their various jobs to the best of their ability. Some we believed to be slackers who " had no stomach for the fight," but who is competent to judge another man's life and motives ? In this connection I met a man about this period who has unknowingly taught me a lesson I shall never forget. I will not mention his name because I feel sure he would not wish it.

An old member of the Regiment, he had his name down for active service only to withdraw it on the eve of the first battalion leaving for the front. It is easy to imagine the contempt of his associates. He was given a commission and was believed to have secured a soft job in some obscure department of the War Office. Occasionally he would visit his Regimental Mess only to be received with what must have been an obvious cold shoulder. He never seemed to mind which added to the derision in which his name was mentioned.

Several years after the War I learned that he was employed in the Secret Service and that half his time was spent in Germany. He had been selected on account of an extraordinarily intimate knowledge of foreign languages and customs. He carried his life in his hands more than any of us. For any mean thought I ever held about him, I am most deeply repentant. He has taught me never to judge any man's courage on outward appearances.

When spring arrived things began to happen. Captain Boyle and Ossy went off to rejoin the first battalion. Then the battalion was moved under canvas in Richmond Park. But both these events were eclipsed by a rumour that the first battalion was to be employed once more as a fighting unit. A draft of officers was to be sent out to join it.

I had received my cue. When that draft went out I was determined to be on it. I was.

My first act was to place myself in the hands of Doc Instone who had become one of my greatest friends since I had joined the Third Battalion Mess. He promised to support me and I sent in my name to the Adjutant as a volunteer. Colonel Evans did not want to let me go but he could not gainsay the medical report which pronounced me fit.

After all, I was quite fit except for a slight weakness in my right arm and shoulder. It is true that the injury to the nerve prevented me from pressing the trigger of my revolver but I got over that by training myself to use my left hand. Every night before I went to bed I used to practise shooting at imaginary objects with my left hand. Two hundred times a night I pressed the trigger until using my left arm was second nature.

On the 24th May, 1916, eight of us left Waterloo *en route* for the first battalion.

CHAPTER THREE

I RETURN TO THE LINE

MY reception by the first battalion left nothing to be desired. The eight of us comprising the draft of officers from England had scarcely put up at the Hotel de France at Hesdin, when we heard a clattering of hooves in the courtyard. Colonel Treffry and Captain, now Major, Boyle had called to welcome us. The Colonel's greeting was characteristically to the point.

" Well, Bombo, you've arrived in the nick of time. I want a battalion bombing officer. Get going at once and train me a platoon of bombers."

I started work the following morning. I had a free hand to do what I liked and I was determined to raise a platoon as efficient as the one which had been wiped out with me in Sanctuary Wood. There was one slight disappointment. The organisation of the battalion no longer provided for a bombing platoon as a separate unit. The bombers normally did Company duty and were only to be used as a bombing platoon when occasion demanded. This meant that I had no individual command. I was attached to Headquarters although I was also appointed to B Company as a Company officer.

There was plenty to do. During the period the battalion was employed as an officers' training corps no one had thought about bombs at all. I was starting at the beginning. Fortunately the weather was perfect.

Not a drop of rain to interfere with progress. By the end of June the battalion had possessed a platoon with a thorough knowledge of bombing and trench-clearing.

As all the world knows the big British push on the Somme started on the first of July. We got a dim echo of it in the form of long strings of motor ambulances bringing down the wounded to hospitals improvised in marquees. The sight made me long to go back to the line and try conclusions once more with Master Fritz.

Rumour, which had been very active ever since I rejoined the Regiment, fructified a few days later. On the eighth of July we left the quiet little town of Hesdin for the front. A four days' march which severely tried all ranks, especially those who were experiencing active service conditions for the first time, brought us to Bouvigny Wood, a short distance behind Souchez.

We were to join the sixty-third, or Royal Naval Division which had recently returned from Gallipoli. They were very greatly depleted in numbers and, owing to the conditions under which they were first mobilised, had no reserve on which they could call. It was proposed to reorganise the R.N.D. proper into two Brigades whilst an Army Brigade would be formed to bring the Division to full strength. The Army Brigade consisted of the 4th Bedfordshires, the 7th Royal Fusiliers, the 8th Dublin Fusiliers and ourselves.

Whilst the Division was forming, the battalion was employed on fatigues. It was very interesting to look back a year and compare my state now that I was an officer. Not that I had by any means a softer time. Actually I was working considerably harder. The difference lay in the increased comfort at the end of the day.

I was engaged in training a second bombing platoon from which casualties in the bombers could be made up. I also lectured to each of the four companies in turn so that every man in the battalion should have a rudimentary knowledge of bombs, and their employment. Further than this I arranged that every man in the battalion threw two live bombs in an actual trench that I had prepared. In this way I hoped to get them all quite familiar with a weapon of which so many were scared simply because they did not understand it.

Colonel Treffry was delighted with the work I was putting in. He was intensely proud of the Regiment and was always ready to sanction anything that would tend to make it more efficient. He was dining one night with the Brigadier shortly after I reported that every man had thrown his two live grenades. In course of conversation the Brigadier asked him whether any of his men was experienced in the handling of bombs.

" All of them," replied the Colonel with a delighted twinkle in his eye.

Nevertheless, I fell from grace one day with a crash. Some of our new officers had been up the line for trench experience. One of them returned with a steel helmet which he presented to the Colonel as a souvenir. So far we had not been issued with our tin hats. They had only just been adopted for use in the Army and were still a novelty. The Colonel was delighted, and, unbeknown to me, hung his trophy on a nail behind the orderly room door.

On the day in question I had an argument with a brother officer as to whether a steel helmet would stop a revolver bullet at close quarters. I said it would ; he protested that the bullet would pierce the steel. We had reached a deadlock when I had a brain-wave.

" I know there's a tin hat hanging up in the orderly room," I said. " Let's take it down on the range and try it."

Without more ado I fetched the hat in blissful ignorance of its ownership, and, placing it on a post, retired twenty-five paces, the distance agreed upon. My shot hit it fair and square at a spot which would have been in the centre of the forehead of anyone wearing it. It spun round a couple of times. When it came to rest it bore a dent about the size of a man's fist. The fellow with whom I had the argument agreed that I had won my point and I replaced the hat where I found it.

There was a terrific hullabaloo when the Colonel discovered the damage. I was nowhere to be found. I had received a timely warning and had gone out for a walk. The C.O. ordered the armourer sergeant to knock out the dent. The armourer heated the helmet red-hot in one of the cookers, tapped it with his hammer, and —put his hammer right through it. Sublime bathos! Within a week several large crates arrived and everybody in the battalion had a tin hat to himself. Before then I had apologised and been forgiven.

The weather still remained nice and fine. I used to sleep out under a tree in preference to having my bed made up in a hut. One night I was awakened by having my face licked. I sat up in my flea-bag and found two large dogs standing over me. One was a retriever and the other a sheep dog. They were homeless and promptly adopted me as their master. As long as we remained in Bouvigny Wood they never left me, night or day. At night they made a habit of sleeping on my feet; during the day they followed me about wherever I went. I have always loved dogs and I was delighted to have them, but there are occasions when two large animals can be an embarrassment.

I well remember the first battalion church parade after their arrival. I thought I had left them safely shut up in my hut. But no sooner were we drawn up in a hollow square with the C.O. in his place ready to take the service than my two pals arrived. In joyous bounds they sprang up around me pleased to have discovered where I had hidden myself. They strongly disapproved of the troops singing the first hymn and barked vociferously. That finished the Colonel.

" Mr. Pollard, will you kindly take those damned dogs off the parade and yourself with them."

It nearly broke my heart when we moved off to the trenches and I had to leave them behind. I gave them to a fellow in a heavy howitzer battery who promised to take care of them. He had to tie them up to prevent them following me. It was impossible for me to take them or I would have done so. I named one of them Mills after the Mills bomb, and the other Hales after the rifle grenade.

So far I had not myself been in the trenches except for a couple of visits of a few hours. The battalion, which consisted largely of fellows without previous experience, was being inured to the line by degrees, the same as when we first went in at Neuve Eglise. It was a very quiet part of the line and I was more usefully employed training my bombers.

But now the Division was formed and we were to commence our regular tours of duty. We first went in as a battalion at a place called Calonne. Three Companies held the front line with one in support. The Company on the left occupied a trench that ran through a slag heap. It was known as the burning bing because some form of internal combustion kept it constantly hot. The men used to parboil their mess-tins merely by leaving them standing on the slag. Behind the right Company stood another slag heap, ninety feet high. The engineers had cut a tunnel through it which formed part of the communication trench.

It was here that I first encountered deep dug-outs made forty feet below the surface of the ground. They were an undoubted acquisition to trench life, if only for the moral effect. In the line in 1915, one was never away from the possibility that a shell might land on one at any time. Now those off duty could sleep in peace secure in the knowledge that their shelters were shell-proof.

Not that we suffered much from shelling in this section of the line. Neither side showed any great artillery activity. To make up for it Fritz strafed us daily with trench mortars. The missiles they were using were of two kinds. One, which consisted of a steel shell crammed with high explosive, was known as a rum jar because of its shape. The other was nick-named a pine-apple, partly on account of its shape and partly because of the steel serrations which were formed on its body. Both were equally deadly if they succeeded in landing in the trench.

To counter them each Company posted a sentry provided with a whistle. Three blasts meant that the danger was to the right ; two blasts to the left ; one, that it was coming straight over. When the warning sounded the troops moved along the trench to another traverse. In this way we suffered very few casualties.

From the very first day I thirsted to reply. Why should the Hun have things all his own way ? I found some rifle racks which took six rifles each. By tying all the triggers together with string, I succeeded in firing them all at once. In each rifle I fixed a rifle grenade and pointed my engine of fearfulness towards where I had seen the pine-apples start. I provided each of the three Companies with a similar machine and gave orders that the bombers were to fire not less than two hundred rifle grenades per day per Company. After a few tries we got the range ; then we proceeded to send over two coveys of rifle grenades every time Fritz pitched us one of his rum jars or pine-apples.

Six hundred rifle grenades per day ! My requisitions to the Brigade bombing officer were terrific. After a few days he asked me to ease up. His supply was unequal to my demand.

I had some great fun one day with a rum jar. It was a dud, and I wanted to take out the detonator ; empty out the sixty pounds of high explosive and, having rendered it innocuous, keep it as a souvenir. I was sitting on the fire step, the rum jar between my knees, working at it with a spanner, when I heard the Commanding Officer's voice at the other side of the traverse.

" We are now coming to the part of the line held by C Company," he was saying.

Accompanied by the Adjutant he was conducting the C.O. and Adjutant of the relieving battalion round the position. Suddenly his voice tailed off in the middle of a sentence. There was a moment's horrified silence. Then a scuffle as the party retired behind the safety of the traverse.

" Bombo ! " called the Colonel. " Put that thing down at once and come here ! "

I meekly obeyed.

" What do you think you are doing ? " he demanded.

" I was just taking the detonator out of a rum jar, sir," I explained.

" Well, go back and pick it up and throw it over the parapet. Just as it is ! "

" But, sir——"

" Do as I tell you," he interrupted my protest. " Do you want to blow us all to smithereens ? "

I could not help laughing as I did as I was told. Once I had succeeded in removing the detonator, it would have been less harmful than a full bottle of its namesake. The C.O. never did have a proper appreciation of bombs.

It was good to be back in the line again. One felt one was pulling one's weight for the Country, doing the right thing. I thoroughly enjoyed it. After a nine months' gap the knowledge that the Huns were just opposite waiting for an opportunity to kill me if I gave them a chance added a spice to life which I had missed.

I gave them a sitting chance one night if only they had been quick enough to seize it. I had decided to take the opportunity of being in a quiet part of the line to accustom myself to finding my way about in No

Man's Land. I had often been out to examine our wire entanglements in Captain Boyle's company. I had also been out quite a lot on my own when I was a corporal at the top of the Ypres Salient. But now I was an officer I was more ambitious. I wanted to examine Fritz's wire as well as ours.

The first time I went out I relied on a compass for my bearings. I took two men with me : Sergeant Harrison, nicknamed " Bomber," a New Zealander who had been a member of my original bombing platoon ; and Reggie Hughesdon, my runner, whose duty it was to accompany me wherever I went. We started out in single file, crawling on our stomachs. I went first and " Bomber " Harrison brought up the rear. On this first occasion we were only out for experience. We certainly got it in that after crawling for some twenty minutes we found ourselves back in our own lines a few hundred yards from where we started. The attraction of the wire entanglements had proved too much for my pocket compass.

We gave it up for that night, but the following night I made another attempt without a compass. I thought it would be quite easy to get my bearings from the big slag heaps in the vicinity of our trench. Half way across No Man's Land I looked back only to realise that a slag heap looks one thing when one is standing beside it in daylight and quite another when one is lying on the ground some distance away at night. However, I persevered, and after crawling about for about an hour and a half we fetched up against a line of barbed wire. We were all three tired of crawling on our tummies and rose thankfully to our feet. It was only then that I realised that the wire was of an entirely different make from that to which I was accustomed. We had completely lost our way and were standing outside the Hun trench.

Realisation came in a flash. But before we could

move a loud voice hailed us in German. Bang ! Some-one fired a rifle.

Discretion is sometimes the better part of valour.

" Come on, you fellows ! " I cried.

We turned and ran like stags. About fifty yards from the wire we tumbled into a convenient shell-hole. I knew what was going to happen. A Very Light flared in the sky. Bang ! Zunk ! Two bombs burst on the spot where we had stood a few moments before. Brrrrrrr ! A machine-gun broke into a staccato rattle. We stayed where we were for half an hour or so until things had calmed down and then crawled back home. Fritz had missed his opportunity. One of his sentries had not been sufficiently on the alert.

I learned a number of things from that patrol. The necessity of arranging some signal so that I could easily find my way back ; the difficulty the men experienced in crawling with their rifles ; the ease with which one could approach an enemy position under cover of night. But mostly I realised how secure Fritz felt in his position.

His wire entanglements were infinitely superior to ours. There had been no attack in this part of the line for over a year, and I suspect the Hun had grown careless through the absence of any particular threat against him.

Could he have seen the mouth of a certain sinister opening in our trench he would have been considerably more uneasy. A shaft run deep down into the earth. There was a miniature railway which carried down huge balks of timber and brought back loads of soil. Men toiled day and night like ants burrowing under the ground. They were a company of miners of the Royal Engineers and they were constructing a mine under the enemy's position.

The War under the earth has a history all its own. It was waged incessantly by men who knew their business but who carried out their daily job with the possibility always hanging over them of being blown to eternity at any moment. Mining did not merely consist of constructing a straightforward shaft. The enemy were also at work building a counter-shaft. Those whose duty it was to listen could often hear the other side working a few feet away from them. Then it became a race against time. Whoever was ready first blew a counter-mine which not only destroyed the enemy shaft but also any of the enemy who happened to be in it at the time. It was a deadly business.

The most famous mine constructed during the War was the British mine which blew up Hill 60. It was a mile and a half long and took two years to make. Throughout the whole period the German engineers were working against it, trying to discover the position of the main shaft and destroy it. Many side shafts were run off and blown to counter the enemy's activities. In the end the British won and Hill 60, the position of which had been gauged to a yard, no mean feat of calculation in itself, went up in a cloud of dust, stones and remnants of human bodies. In addition to the normal garrison, there was a German labour battalion at work on the hill at the time some nine hundred strong. All were destroyed.

I well remember one of the counter mines being blown in July 1915. We were in some trenches to the right of the Ypres Salient. It was about eleven o'clock at night, and I was standing on the fire step of the trench talking to one of the sentries. All of a sudden there was an ear-splitting explosion. I knew at once that it was not caused by a shell. The sound was deadened as though one had some cotton-wool in one's ears. For a moment the parapet rocked violently. Peering through the night I saw what appeared to be a black cloud rise slowly from the earth. The next instant stones and dirt rained down all about us.

Pandemonium broke loose in both lines of trenches. Every rifle and machine-gun opened fire simultaneously. I don't imagine that anyone knew quite what he was firing at. Everyone obeyed the common war instinct to loose off his rifle when in doubt of what was taking place. The shindy lasted for about half an hour and then died away.

There was nothing very dreadful in that experience, but I have often tried to picture what my feelings would be if I knew that the enemy were attempting to mine the trench underneath me. I suppose the answer is that one never does know until it is too late. Otherwise one would withdraw oneself and one's troops to another position. It is the one form of warfare to which there is no counter except by running a mine in opposition. The infantry are helpless.

We did not stay at Calonne long enough to be in the fun when the mine was blown. We only did the one trip before we were withdrawn and entrained for an unknown destination. Rumour had it that we were going south to the Somme.

CHAPTER FOUR

NIGHT PATROLS

RUMOUR, as usual, proved wrong. We went south, but not to the Somme. For the time being we encamped at Marquay, in the neighbourhood of St. Pol. We had scarcely got settled when Fate dealt me one of the heaviest buffets I had ever received in my life. I received news from home that my only brother had been killed in action.

For the moment it quite knocked me out. Before the War I had always looked to him to give me a lead. His four years seniority in age had made him so much my elder brother. Now he was gone I realised how much he had always meant to me. It is one thing to be a fire-eater oneself, enjoying the thrill of risking one's life. It is quite another to know that one's own flesh and blood is in danger and that one can do nothing to help.

It came especially hard in that his commission was gazetted within a few days of his death. Had he lived another week he would have gone back to England for a six months' course at an officers' training school. Even so he might have succumbed later in the War, but he would first have enjoyed the greater comfort that life as an officer would have brought him.

I had fixed it all up before I left England. My brother's leave came just before I was due for the front. I took him before the Colonel of our reserve battalion and persuaded him to offer him a commission in his old Regiment. His desertion was forgiven in view of his subsequent service at the front. He was to be welcomed back. I saw that all the papers were filled in ; there was nothing to do but wait.

I felt so deeply for my mother. Now my brother was gone all her worry would be concentrated on me. I was faced with a momentous decision. Ought I to rest on the laurels I had already earned and get a soft job which would keep me out of the danger of bullets and shells, or did my duty to my Country come before my respect for my mother's feelings ? My own inclination went naturally towards staying at the front in order to revenge my brother's death. I felt that never again would I pity any of the enemy. Rather would I do my utmost to kill as many as possible. But one has sometimes to put one's own feelings on one side. My Country or my mother ? In the end my Country won. I reasoned that, were we defeated, my mother's state would be infinitely worse. Therefore it behoved me to do my utmost to assure my Country's victory. In that way I would be serving both my Country and my mother. But I made a mental reservation that I would get leave to go home and see her as soon as possible.

At the end of September we moved to Mailly-Maillet and went into the line in the Redan sector. Things were very much more active here than they had been at Calonne. The whole neighbourhood was alive with artillery and it was very evident that the Staff were making preparations for a big attack.

The Commanding Officer sent for me as soon as we had taken over from the outgoing battalion. The command had now devolved on Major, now Colonel Boyle. Colonel Treffry had been invalided home. " Ossy," now Major Osmond, was second-in-command. He and Colonel Boyle were a wonderful pair to fight under. I found them in the Headquarters dug-out, both poring over a large-scale map of the district.

" I want you to make a raid to-night, Pollard," boomed the Colonel, in his deep voice. " Corps want us to identify the troops opposite. There's a sap-head with a machine-gun and six men in it. Make any arrangements you like but bring me a Hun."

" Very good, sir," I replied. " May I have a look at the map ? "

" Of course. Here's the spot."

The Colonel made a mark with his pencil and handed me the map. The German front line was an average of some three hundred yards distant. At one part, on the right of our battalion front, their trench came out towards us in a distinct triangle. The sap-head I was to raid was at the apex.

" I shall want to go out and have a look at it," I remarked.

" There's no need for that," said the Colonel. " It's all done for you. An officer from the battalion we relieved made a reconnaissance last night."

He handed me a copy of the report. It read convincingly—a little too convincingly. The man who wrote it might have been actually in the sap-head at the time. It seemed to me that his description of the place was too full of detail.

" All the same, sir, I should like to see the place myself before I take on the responsibility of a raid," I protested.

The Colonel pooh-poohed my sense of caution. It was imperative that the raid be carried out as soon as possible. I was only making double work when a satisfactory report was already available. I remained firm and in the end he gave way. His tone showed that he was a trifle disappointed in me. I had not so much dash as he had given me credit for.

Immediately I left him I set about making arrangements for my reconnaissance. This time I took three men with me. My runner, Reggie Hughesdon, who, although only nineteen, was full of pluck and grit. He was a great asset in that he was a remarkably accurate bomb-thrower. Now that my wounded shoulder precluded me from throwing bombs myself, I was always glad to know that one of my followers was capable of dropping a bomb just where I wanted it.

The other two who made up my party were Privates Fishbourne and Mars. Fishbourne was a man of fifty-one who hailed from somewhere in the Australian bush. He had lived a pretty hard life and was as tough as they are made. In every respect he was thoroughly dependable.

Mars had spent a large portion of his life in South America in the wide open spaces. He had been employed as a wire rider, which meant that for days on end he had had to ride round the miles and miles of wire fences which prevent the huge herds of cattle from straying outside the boundaries of the hacienda to which they belong. A kick from a mule had knocked his nose on one side and badly scarred his face. He had no conception whatever of what fear meant.

With the experience I had gained at Calonne I relieved them of their rifles and armed them with revolvers which I borrowed from the Lewis-gun officer. Each man was a trained bomber and carried two Mills bombs in his pocket. I knew there would be a moon and, to make quite sure that our faces would not reflect the moonlight and give us away, we rubbed them over with burnt cork. We looked a terrifying company.

I was taking extra care over my precautions because I had not the slightest intention of confining my activities to a reconnaissance. The Colonel's attitude had stung me to a determination to go full out to capture a Hun that night. I had not said a word to a soul, not even the men who were going with me. I was going to have a look first, and if the situation was anything like the one outlined in the report, I meant to have a stab at laying out the machine-gun team, saving one alive for the Colonel.

We started from our front line trench in single file. After crawling some fifty yards I chose a large shell-hole and, gathering my followers round me, explained the situation. They were all game as I knew they would be.

We moved forward again in the form of a diamond. I went first with Reggie about twenty yards behind me. Fishbourne and Mars were some ten yards away on either flank. The moon was nearly full and shed its ghostly radiance on a scene of terrible desolation. A thick black line some hundred and fifty yards ahead marked the position of the Hun barbed-wire entanglements. Looking back I could make out a similar line in front of our own trench. Between were innumerable shell-holes of all sizes, some half full of water, some newly made ; all evidence of the terrific number of shells which had been fired in that neighbourhood.

I had not proceeded very far before I felt something yield and scrunch under me. It was the skeleton of a corpse, its bones picked clean by the army of rats which scavenged the battlefields. The rags of a tunic still covered its nakedness. I felt in the pockets to try and discover some means of identification, but they were empty. Someone had been before me. Further on I found another ; then another and another. The ground was scattered with them. They were the bodies of those slain in the terrible fighting at the beginning of July. All were British.

We were now nearer the German line than our own, and I could make out the triangle at the top of which our objective was situated. The night was so bright that very few Very Lights were being used. When one was fired we all kept perfectly still. Fritz might spot us moving against the ground, but whilst we were motionless we were invisible.

A low hist from Fishbourne on my left brought me to an abrupt stop. With infinite caution I crawled over to where he was lying. He pointed towards the triangle.

" I can see something moving," he whispered.

I followed the direction of his finger. Something was undoubtedly moving backwards and forwards. It looked exactly as though men were passing and repassing one another.

" There's the machine-gun, too," said Fishbourne.

It certainly looked as though a dark barrel were pointing towards us, and I began to think the report of my predecessor was correct. My heart beat a trifle faster. We should be in the middle of it in a few minutes.

" Make a slight detour and creep in from the left. Mars will do the same on the right. Hughesdon and I will move straight forward. I'll fire one shot as a signal for us all to close in together."

I crawled across and told Mars; then brought Reggie up on my flank. We were now in the form of a crescent slowly closing in on our unconscious quarry. My revolver was held steady in my hand. At the first sign that we were spotted I meant to open fire.

We had got within ten yards of the sap-head before I realised we were stalking an enemy who did not exist. Tall grasses waving in the wind had supplied the illusion of men moving to and fro; the machine-gun was an uprooted post which was lying across the parapet. The sap was deserted.

We closed in right up to the parapet. It was still necessary to move with extreme caution in case we were seen from the main line trench. The sap was filled in with thick barbed-wire entanglements. Lying underneath, sole guardian of the outpost, lay the grim figure of a dead German. He was in a state of decomposition, which showed the length of time he had been in possession. The fact that he was there at all made it evident that the sap had been evacuated in a great hurry.

I had vindicated my determination to reconnoitre the position before making the raid on another man's report. If I had organised the show and taken a dozen or so men over the top, we might easily have suffered several casualties from stray bullets and got nothing in return. Colonel Boyle was the first to agree with my point of view when I made my report on our return.

" It's a good job you insisted, Pollard." He smiled.

It was not much perhaps, but it was enough for me.

The following night I went out again with the same party. I wanted to try and find another place where a raid might be possible. We moved forward fairly quickly to the sap-head. Here I adopted my diamond formation with the idea that if one of us was hit, the other three would be sufficiently scattered to stand a chance of escape.

We crept down the left side of the sap towards the Hun main line. Somewhere in the distance a Very Light flared into the sky. We lay motionless, but, by its light, I could see that the Hun wire was in a very poor state of repair. Our artillery had played havoc with it, but, at the same time, it was very unlike Master Fritz's usual habits to neglect to repair the damage. I began to think hard. Had he left those gaps through neglect, or did he need them for his troops to pour through in an attack on our line ? Whatever else I did I must make sure of his intentions before I returned home.

Nearer and nearer we crept to the wire. Everything was deathly still. Except for an occasional Very Light there was no sign of life. I reached a gap in the entanglements and signalled my three men to join me. Leaving them to cover my advance I crawled slowly, with the greatest care not to make a noise, through the gap towards the Hun parapet. Nothing moved ; no one challenged me. I reached the parapet and put my head over the top. The trench was deserted.

Here was a stupendous discovery. In preparation for the big attack which everyone felt to be imminent, our artillery were daily sending over hundreds and hundreds of shells with the dual idea of smashing the Hun wire entanglements and beating down the enemy *moral*. And, all the time, the wily Fritz had withdrawn to a position in rear on which our guns had not registered, and in which they were probably laughing up their dirty field-grey sleeves.

" But what about the man firing the Very Lights ? " asked Mars, when I had motioned my three stalwarts to join me in the Hun front line. " I'm certain some were fired from this trench."

He may have been right, but although we searched along the trench for some distance, we found no trace of any Hun whatsoever. The trench was full of mud and all falling to pieces. It had obviously not been occupied for some time. It is possible that we were deceived into thinking that the star-shells came from the front line when they really came from the second by the various twists and turns of the position. Anyway, I did not find brother Hun that night or either of the two following, although I looked diligently for him.

We did not go back home immediately. Instead, I had a brain wave. We would find out exactly where the enemy were and, at the same time, give him a bit of a scare.

There were two enormous shell-holes running into one another immediately in front of the trench. The four of us got into these and lined up. I got out my note-book and drew a rough sketch of the line ; the others took out their Mills bombs and laid them down in front of them.

At a given signal they drew out the safety pins and threw all the bombs as far as they could towards the German position. So far the night had been fairly quiet. We were to disturb the silence in no uncertain manner.

Zunk ! Bang ! Zunk ! Bang ! Zunk ! Zunk ! the bombs exploded one after the other. There was a moment's stupefied silence and then hell broke loose.

Rifles, machine-guns, field-guns, howitzers all started firing at the same moment. My three got well down in the shell-hole. I lay with my chin above the edge and filled in, as accurately as possible, the positions of the various machine-guns as exposed by the flashes, on my improvised map. When we got back I sent it to Corps so that the artillery could strafe them if they thought fit.

The riot proved conclusively that the Hun front line trench was unoccupied. There was not a single flash from it as far as the eye could see.

We were all hugely delighted with the result of our strategy. That is, we were at first. The one element we had overlooked was our own artillery. They had been warned of my patrol before I went out, but they forgot all about that when Fritz opened fire. Within one minute of the Hun starting, our counter batteries were busy replying. Shells burst round us thick and fast, and we began to wonder how long it would be before we were hoist on our own petard. The show lasted for three-quarters of an hour and then died away almost as suddenly as it had commenced. We lost no time in creeping back to the safety of our trench.

I spent most of the following day racking my brains for a stunt which would deliver a Hun into my hands. By dusk I believed I had evolved a water-tight scheme. We had a fellow in the battalion who had lived fourteen years in Bavaria. He could of course speak German like a native. I decided to use him as a decoy.

My plan was perfectly simple. I got a Hun uniform and dressed my man in it complete with Hun steel helmet. Then I proposed to take him over No Man's Land where he was to crawl along in front of the Hun trench as though he was seriously wounded and groan. He was to continue groaning until he had attracted the attention of a Hun sentry, who would naturally call out to know who he was and what he was doing. Of course there was a possibility that he might shoot first and enquire afterwards, but I did not tell my decoy that. My man was to reply that he belonged to the 82nd Prussian Regiment, who were known to be opposite the troops on our left ; that he had been wounded on a patrol the previous evening ; that he had spent the day in a shell-hole, and was now lost.

I estimated that if he acted in a sufficiently realistic manner—his German was above suspicion—the Huns would send out a stretcher party to carry him in. That would be my cue. I should be waiting in a convenient shell-hole with my band of desperadoes and would fall on the stretcher party as they emerged from their trench. If we did not manage to secure one alive we should be extremely unlucky. To make assurance doubly sure I arranged for a platoon to be stationed half-way across No Man's Land for my support. My old friend Captain " Ted " Ellis, now commanding A Company insisted on supplying the platoon and intended to take charge of it himself. I am quite sure that if the principal character had not let us down the affair would have been a cinch.

I rehearsed him thoroughly in his part until he was perfect. I dressed him in his uniform. I made all the arrangements. We were all ready to commence when Fritz started to shell.

It was nothing very much. Small stuff, and directed, not at us but at somewhere behind our lines. But we were on our way up to the front trench at the time and the moral effect of those few shells was too much for my stool-pigeon.

I was leading the way with him following immediately behind me. For some time I thought I heard a noise like subdued castanets. When I eventually turned round I discovered what it was. His teeth were chattering and he was shaking as though he had an ague. He was quite incapable of speaking in English let alone posing as a wounded German. The show was a flop before it had started. And I had wasted a double tot of rum on him too. There was nothing for it but to send him back to his Company.

The four of us went over to the Hun front line and crawled towards the line they were holding as far as we dared. We were unable to get right up to it as the moon was nearly full and the ground was almost as light as day. It is an extraordinary thing that we were able to go as far as we did. Our only hope was to catch a hun patrol similar to ourselves, or to surprise a party working on the wire entanglements, but again we were unlucky.

My friend Percy Lewis was killed the following day by a shell in the fourth line. During the time I was home wounded he had been given a job in the Orderly Room as a clerk where he had been ever since. It was his turn to accompany the battalion into the line or he would have been left safely in the transport field. My only consolation was that he was killed outright.

I did not feel it as much as I had expected. I think my brother's death had hardened me. No one else seemed to matter now that he was gone. Never again would I feel such a sharp pang of infinite regret. My nature was becoming callous.

I went out on patrol again that night. Again we met with no luck. In fact I met with very definite bad luck. I pricked my knee on a spike of the Hun barbed wire. It was old and rusty. When I returned to the trench I lay down to snatch a few hours' sleep. When I awakened my knee was the size of a football bladder, and so stiff I could scarcely bend it. I saw the doctor and told him how it happened. He could see I had water on the knee but thought perhaps it might turn septic from the rusty wire. He despatched me forthwith to hospital.

I had not had the luck to get my Hun but I think I damned well deserved one.

CHAPTER FIVE

I PLAY TRUANT

IT was the middle of October when I was sent to hospital. If the attack which was on everyone's tongue was to take place before the winter set in, it would have to be soon. Judging from the two winters that had passed since the commencement of the War, there would be very little fighting during the cold weather. At least, so I thought at the time. Subsequent events proved that my prediction was incorrect.

I went to hospital with the fixed idea of getting my knee well as soon as possible and rejoining the battalion in time for the scrap. I was extremely annoyed at having to be away at all at that time when everything pointed to the affair coming off any day. But the medicos were absolute. The battalion doctor would not take the chance of my knee not causing trouble.

The field-dressing station never even examined me. I was put straight into an ambulance and taken to the Casualty Clearing Station. Here I went to bed and my knee was thoroughly overhauled. The result of the examination was that I was marked for the base. I argued and implored but the authorities were adamant. They too were expecting the attack and they needed every bed cleared in preparation.

So down to the base I went; this time to a hospital at Wimereux. I arrived in the middle of the night and was duly put to bed. Later, the Night Matron in charge of the hospital came round to see that I was all right. I recognised her immediately. She was the pretty Sister with whom I had made friends when at Nantes in 1914.

She was as pleased to see me as I was to see her. Naturally we both had a great deal of news as we had not met for two years. She could not very well stay in the ward talking to me without making all the other patients jealous. For three days we could only converse in fits and starts. Then we had a joint brain wave.

By this time my knee had been attended to and the swelling was beginning to abate. I was allowed to be up so long as I did not use my leg too much. It is very irksome lying in bed when one is feeling absolutely fit. I used to walk about the ward and adjacent corridors with the aid of a stick. One evening, after the night staff had come on duty, I ventured upstairs and visited the Night Matron's office.

I did not stay very long as she was busy making preparations for the night. But I arranged to go back later for a chat when things had settled down.

Lights out was at ten o'clock. After that hour every one was supposed to be asleep. About a quarter-past ten I slipped quietly out of bed and into my dressing-gown. The stairs were deserted and I reached the office without being seen. Sister and one of the nurses who was a great friend of hers were enjoying a rest and a cigarette. I joined them and we made a merry trio. About midnight, I returned noiselessly to bed, whilst they got on with their work.

After that my visit became a nightly occurrence. It was great sport. I was rapidly getting better and was able to take short walks along the cliffs by the sea. Sister and her friend often accompanied me. They made my stay in hospital a great pleasure.

I had told her all about my brother having been killed and how worried I was about my mother. She said she thought she could wangle me some special leave through one of the hospital chiefs who was a great friend of hers. At first I declined. I ought to rejoin the battalion as soon as possible.

The old question was uppermost in my mind. My duty or my mother. It is extremely difficult to look back on a situation from the distance of years and say what course one would take did one have one's chance over again. I really believe though, judging from the way I acted on other occasions, that had I known for certain when my Regiment was going into action, I should have remained firm and hurried back up the line. But I was not sure. Six weeks had now passed since the word attack was first mentioned and nothing had happened. I thought it quite probable that any action on a large scale would be postponed until the Spring. I was desperately keen to see my mother. I asked Sister to go ahead. She got me a special leave warrant without any difficulty.

Our party did not break up on the last night before I left for England until later than usual. I had smuggled in a bottle of wine with which to celebrate and we kept things going until nearly one o'clock. Quietly as usual I returned to my bed. A figure was waiting by it. As I approached I saw that it was the junior nurse who was on night duty in the ward.

" Where have you been ? " she asked sternly. " You've been away from your bed night after night. I haven't said anything before because I did not want to get you into a row, but this is too much. Past one o'clock indeed ! I shall report you to Matron."

She flounced off and I crept humbly into bed. Ten minutes later she reappeared followed by the girl with whom I had spent the last three hours. Without the vestige of a smile Sister admonished me severely for having been a naughty boy, and told me that it was not to occur again. I gravely promised to mend my ways.

F

We both knew whilst we were speaking that it could not happen again—worse luck !

She was a great sport. Unfortunately I have never seen her since. I must not give her name. She is a very famous personage. I wonder if she remembers ?

I crossed to England on the first of November. My mother was delighted to see me, especially so as my leave was unexpected. She was wonderfully cheerful in view of my brother's recent death. I know it did her good to have me at home even for so short a time as a fortnight.

Of course I made an excuse to see the girl who still occupied all my thoughts. She was very nice to me and once again I began to entertain foolish hopes. Not that I said a word to break our contract. Outwardly we were merely friends although she must have known my real feelings towards her were only kept in check by force of will.

I took her out as often as she could get leave from hospital. On my last afternoon we managed to get in a matinée. As we left the theatre the newsboys were crying in the streets. The placards announced, " Big British Push." I had no need to buy a paper. I knew without that. My Regiment had gone into action without me. I had failed in my duty.

The attack started on the thirteenth of November and lasted two days. The battalion covered itself with glory but was very badly cut up. Their casualty list was enormous. And whilst they had been in action I was enjoying myself at the theatre.

I felt very badly about it at the time, although I did not in the least regret the few days I had snatched for my mother's benefit. My feelings were a mixture of hurt pride and bitter regret. I should have liked both to see my mother and to rejoin the battalion in time for the show. Looking back in after years I doubt very much whether I should have been able to get back to the battalion in time even if I had forgone the leave. One had to follow the Army routine of proceeding to a base camp on discharge from hospital and waiting until the spirit moved the authorities to forward one up the line. I returned to France on the fourteenth of November but it was not until the thirtieth that I received my instructions to leave the Base at Havre. Assuming that I should have been the same time, even had I gone direct to the Base from hospital and I should have missed the attack anyhow.

I had one rather amusing adventure whilst I was marooned at the base. Being an old soldier I did as little work as possible thereby falling into the Adjutant's bad books. One day I saw my name in orders for duty as Orderly Officer on the following day. Now the first job of an Orderly Officer is to inspect the men's breakfasts, a tedious proceeding which necessitates getting up at a very unearthly hour. The result is, or was then, that very often the Orderly Officer left the breakfasts to be inspected by the Orderly Sergeant and snatched a few extra precious minutes of sleep.

On the day in question I made an extra effort and got up. I had a strong suspicion that the Adjutant would be on the watch to catch me out and I did not intend to give him an opportunity if I could help it. I found an Orderly Sergeant waiting on the main camp road, and having introduced myself, I told him I was ready to inspect the breakfasts. He led me some distance down the road and then into a men's mess hut. I made my inspection and then went off to my own breakfast with a clear conscience.

Shortly after morning parade I was sent for to the Adjutant's office. The Adjutant frowned at me from behind his desk.

" How was it that you failed to inspect the men's breakfasts this morning, Mr. Pollard ? " he asked nastily.

"I did inspect them, sir," I replied quite truthfully.

"Indeed?" he sneered. "I've made enquiries of the Orderly Sergeant and he tells me he did not have you with him this morning. What have you to say to that?"

"I can only suggest the man's not quite right in the head," I said pertly. I was furiously angry. The idea of taking a sergeant's word before mine.

The Adjutant rang a bell and had the Orderly Sergeant brought into the room.

"That wasn't the Orderly Sergeant who was with me," I said at once. I had never seen the man before.

This rather took the Adjutant aback. Enquiries were made and it was discovered that whilst I was looking for an Orderly Sergeant, the Orderly Sergeant from the next camp was looking for his Orderly Officer. We met and the result was that the breakfasts in the adjoining camp were inspected but not ours. The Adjutant was decent enough to apologise for his mistake although it was perfectly obvious that he had done his best to catch me out. He treated me with considerably more respect afterwards.

I found the battalion resting at Nouvion. Everyone was very cheery and there were a number of tunics wearing bright new ribbon decorations. I had rather a trenchant interview with the Commanding Officer when I went to report my return at Headquarters. He started by enquiring sympathetically after my knee. I explained that it was now quite all right. He then asked me sharply what the devil I meant by getting special leave when I knew there was a possibility of the battalion going into action. I attempted to justify myself by explaining that I had gone home to see my mother.

"Soldiers don't have mothers," said Colonel Boyle bluntly. "Your action was the action of a coward, Pollard."

This was a very bitter pill to swallow from the man who's opinion I valued above all others. Coming on top of the qualms of my own conscience, it plunged me into the depths of misery. I think he appreciated what my true thoughts were for, to tone down his admonition, he made me have tea with him, and told me all about the show and how well everyone had behaved. When I was on the point of leaving he applied a salve to my gall.

" I think perhaps it was as well you weren't with us," he smiled. " You'd most certainly have been killed and then I'd have had to find someone else to do my night patrols. You'll have plenty more opportunities to show what you are made of."

That made me feel a bit better but I knew I should not regain my pride until we returned to the line. To make my position more difficult, everyone was talking about his experiences in the attack and I felt very much out of the conversation. On top of it came a ghastly rumour that the authorities had decided to withdraw us from the Division and turn us once more into an Officers' Training Corps.

There was considerable credence given to this rumour on account of the formation of a Divisional School of Instruction for which all the instructors were supplied by our Regiment. I was detailed as the bombing instructor and took up my duties on the 21st December. I did not mind at all whilst we were out resting as I always hated being entirely idle but I made a mental reservation that my job would only last whilst the battalion remained out of the line.

The School was situated in an old-world château with perfectly glorious grounds. It was a delightful place in which to spend Christmas and we made the most of our opportunity.

A few days later came a counter rumour that we would be returning to the line in a few days. I immediately sent in my resignation from the post of bombing instructor after only six days' work. The Commandant was rather fed up about it but I could not help that.

An interesting sidelight is thrown on my feelings about my duty by a letter I wrote home on the thirtieth of December.

DEAREST MATER,

I hear you have not been very well. I hope you are all right again now. The post is absolutely up the stick, probably owing to Christmas. I have received the footer clothes and the uniform and Perk's cake; all very acceptable. I am at present at the school as I told you and intended to remain here, but really, mater, internal inspiration tells me I must go back up the line when the battalion go. I don't suppose that will be until nearly the end of January so don't start worrying, but I feel it's up to me to go with them. I have sent in my resignation but may be retained until the end of the course. Anyhow, you might wash out addressing me to the school and continue addressing me to the battalion. I am very sorry, mater, but I know you will understand.

I have had some splendid riding lately. Yesterday afternoon I rode into a town about seven miles away. Coming back we had a three mile gallop without a check. Rather splendid! There are two rows of trees by the side of the road with soft earth between them.

Well cheerioh!

The town was Abbeville. I well remember the occasion because I visited a brothel in the street of the red lamps. It was the second and last time in which I was ever in one of these houses of iniquity. I heard that a young officer who had come down to the school for instruction had been fool enough to allow his desires

166

to overcome his self-respect. I followed him into the place and dragged him out. It was quite simple. I asked him whether he had a girl at home who loved him. He said, " Yes." So I said, " How would you feel if she knew you had been in here ? " He came away at once.

They released me to rejoin my battalion during the first week in January. The post of battalion bombing officer had now been done away with and I returned to ordinary company duty. I was put in charge of No. 7 platoon in B Company. My platoon sergeant was Sergeant H. W. Snoad, an extremely efficient soldier. His efficiency was no doubt due in part to the fact that before the War he was one of the private secretaries to the late Lord Northcliffe.

On the 13th January, 1917, the battalion marched out of Nouvion *en route* for the line.

CHAPTER SIX

GRANDCOURT

TOWARDS the end of January 1917, the weather turned bitterly cold. Snow lay on the ground which was frozen as hard as iron. We went into trenches captured from the Bosche just in front of Beaucourt in the valley of the Ancre, the scene of the battalion's attack on the 13th and 14th of November. Fortunately there were plenty of deep dug-outs and we were able to make ourselves fairly snug.

Conditions were far and away better than in the winter of 1914. There were considerably more troops which meant, in theory, that we did not have to spend so much time in the line. We were told that rests would be more frequent and of longer duration. We were to do six weeks up the line and then have six weeks' rest.

Had we simply sat down and remained where we were, I have no doubt that we should have been able to make ourselves extremely comfortable. As it turned out we were kept continually on the move. But nobody foresaw in January the activity in which we were to be involved before the Spring.

An event of considerable importance for me was the arrival of a mascot from the youngest sister of Her whom I adored. It was a small china doll, naked except for a purple ribbon tied round its middle. It had a seraphic expression and bright blue eyes. I christened it Billiken and swore that I would take him with me wherever I went. From that day he accompanied me in my pocket both in the line and out.

On the twenty-ninth of January, Fritz raided one of our listening outposts. My Company was in support and the first we heard about it was a frantic order to stand to. It was a pitch-black night and snowing hard. It was impossible to see more than a few yards ahead.

We were in support. The front line was about four hundred yards in front of us. In front of them again, and about fifty yards apart, were four listening posts in shell-holes. Each consisted of an N.C.O. and ten men with a Lewis gun. An officer was responsible for the four positions.

We heard the story from one of the two survivors left for dead. The Hun party consisted of a Sergeant-Major, armed with an automatic and some thirty men armed with a short mace apiece. They came over in dead silence and under the cloak of the snow storm reached the shell-hole almost before they were discovered. Almost, not quite. An empty drum of Lewis gun ammunition and a number of empty cartridge cases told the story of the defence put up by the tiny garrison. The officer who was in the next shell-hole at the time did not hear a sound until the Lewis gun suddenly opened fire. He hurried across the short distance separating him from the scene of the attack only to find it was all over and the enemy vanished, taking with them the Lewis gun and several of the garrison.

It was jolly bad luck on the officer concerned. I do not see how he could be held responsible on a night like that. The Divisional General thought otherwise and talked about Courts of Enquiry and all sorts of dread inquisitions. I was not yet in a position to make my voice heard in the land or I should have suggested that a senior officer from the Brigade or Division spent a night in one of those shell-holes with the temperature well below freezing point and the snow coming down thick and fast, so that he would be in a position to give the General first-hand evidence on which to estimate the amount of blame that could be hung on to anybody. However, the only person who asked my opinion was the officer himself and I am glad to think I helped him to fight down the bitterness of being accused of having failed in his job.

B Company did not have a turn in the front line that trip. We went back into reserve for a few days and then returned to find that one of the Naval Division battalions had made an attack whilst we were back and had shifted the front line some hundreds of yards forward. We were now on the crest of a hill in front of the Bois d'Hollande. On our right the hill sloped down to the river with Grandcourt on its opposite bank.

My platoon was on the extreme right of the Company. Next to me were C Company, my immediate neighbours being the platoon commanded by Edward Holder, otherwise known as the Ox, an old friend of mine from the days when we were both privates.

I spent the first night in getting the general lay-out of the position. We were in a very shallow trench which had been hastily dug by the troops who made the attack. It was almost impossible to improve it because the ground was so hard, but we kept the troops at work to help their circulations.

The second night I went out on a patrol to examine the Hun line. They were holding the side of a sunken road with practically no wire entanglements to protect them. From this I deduced that they were second-class troops or else the bitter cold was having an effect on their morale. In my experience Master Fritz very seldom failed to make himself as secure against attack as possible.

I only took Reggie Hughesdon with me on this patrol. Fishbourne, my Australian bushranger, was killed in the November show. Mars was also killed, knocked out by one of our own shells which unfortunately fell short in our line. In any case I doubt whether I should have gone out with more than one man. It was tricky work crawling in No Man's Land at any time; with the snow on the ground one was bound to show up even at night time. It was only by moving very slowly and taking advantage of the many shell-holes, that we succeeded in getting across and back without being spotted.

I did get back—to find the Colonel waiting for me in the front trench. He was obviously very excited. He did not even wait for me to jump down into the trench but climbed on to the parapet to meet me.

" I've got a magnificent job for you, Pollard," he boomed. " You're to take a patrol and enter Grandcourt at all costs. At all costs," he reiterated impressively.

I glanced instinctively across at the Hun trench from which I had just returned. The night was frosty and voices are apt to travel in the still air. I did not in the least mind making an attempt on Grandcourt—having something to do would keep me warm at any rate. But I did not want to find a nice little ambush waiting for me through our friends across the way having heard the Colonel's very penetrating voice giving me my orders.

Another interesting point was that I had seen Hun troops in Grandcourt that afternoon. If the Colonel meant me to capture the place, which, knowing him, was not unlikely, there were a great many things I wanted to know. For one thing the River Ancre flowed between me and my objective. There was no bridge in British territory. How was it proposed that I should convey my command across in the teeth of the enemy ?

He cleared that point away almost at once.

" The Air Force have reported that the Huns evacuated Grandcourt at dusk. I want you to confirm what they say before the Marines on the other side of the river find out. It'll be a feather in our caps if we're there first."

"Very good, sir. How do I cross the river?"

The Colonel shrugged his shoulders.

"I must leave that to you, Pollard. I expect you'll find a way. Come and see me when you get back."

He turned away and left me to it. I could make what arrangements I pleased so long as I entered Grandcourt before the Marines. I looked at my watch. It was past one o'clock. I should have to hurry with my arrangements if I were to enter Grandcourt at all that night.

I took my usual patrol of four men. Instead of Fishbourne and Mars I took Lance-Corporal Freter and Lance-Corporal Scharlach. The moon was almost full and, whilst it enabled us to see where we were going, it also made us horribly conspicuous against the snow.

We started off down the hill in single file. Scarcely a hundred yards in front of our position there was a deserted forward trench which had been occupied by a platoon of the Naval Division battalion who preceded us. They were still there—all dead. They had been surprised by the Hun in a counter-attack launched by night and bayoneted to a man. I had heard something about the incident but had forgotten it. Now it came back to me with full force, and at the same time set me thinking. If the Huns had succeeded in surprising that trench they could only have done so from the flank. I tried to visualise what had happened. The British had probably considered themselves invulnerable from the river side. They had possibly not bothered to place a sentry there. The Huns had simply crept up the hill and taken them, either in the flank or even possibly in rear. That meant that there was a way across the river. Well, if Fritz could find one I was damned sure I could, too.

As we carried on down the hill I could not help casting

my mind back to the first time I saw a trench filled with dead men. That was on the 16th June, 1915, when we attacked the Hun in Wye Wood. What a lot of changes had taken place in my life since then. All my old friends were either killed or scattered; new ones had taken their places. Then the battalion was fairly raw; now we were mostly seasoned veterans. But the chief change had taken place in myself.

In June 1915 I was a mere boy looking on life with hopeful optimism, and on war as an interesting adventure. When I saw the Hun corpses killed by our shell-fire I was full of pity for the men so suddenly cut off in their prime. Now I was a man with no hope of the War ending for years. I looked at a trench full of corpses without any sensation whatever. Neither pity nor fear that I might soon be one myself, nor anger against their killers. Nothing stirred me. I was just a machine carrying out my appointed work to the best of my ability.

At the bottom of the hill there was normally marsh land. Now it was frozen over—fortunately for us. It would have been terribly heavy work crossing it if it had been mud and water. I was following the tracks made by the Hun raiding party. These brought me to the waters edge, and I saw at once how they had succeeded in crossing. Two railway lines laid side by side made a passable though rather rickety bridge.

So far we had seen no signs of life on the opposite bank. What should we find when we reached it? Had the Hun really retired or was he now watching our approach from some concealed position, waiting for us to fall into his hands? We should soon know. I made sure my revolver was ready for instant action and climbed on to the railway lines. As soon as I had crossed I took up a position behind a ruined wall to cover the others, and signalled them to follow me. Reggie came last and slipping on the frosty metal fell into the water up to his waist. Two minutes later I had discovered what the Colonel wanted to know. Grandcourt was unoccupied.

So far so good, but neither Colonel Boyle nor I would be satisfied with that. We should both want to know if the Hun had left Grandcourt, where was he now ?

I had just completed a tour round the ruined village and made sure it was quite deserted when one of my followers reported that he thought he saw a man lying in the snow behind the village. It certainly looked like one and we set off to investigate. When we got up to it we found it was only a large log of wood. In itself it is of no importance ; its significance lies in the fact that it was the means of tempting me out into the open.

I was on the point of turning back to the village when a line of dark figures suddenly appeared on the skyline. There were about twenty or thirty of them. My trouble was that I did not know whether they were friends or foes. So clear was the night that we could see them distinctly at a distance of some hundred and fifty yards. They saw us almost at the same moment and immediately went down on the ground.

Here was the deuce of a dilemma. Twenty or thirty rifle barrels were pointing straight at us. If we turned to run we should not get very far. If we walked towards them and they were Huns we should be putting our necks into a noose. I had to make an instantaneous decision.

I determined at once to go towards them. If they were friends, all well and good. If they were enemies there would be a pretty little scrap. I instructed my party to hold their hands above their heads. All's fair in war, and the ruse would enable us to get near enough to them to give us the chance of a fight. Also, we might encounter a shell-hole on the way into which we could jump. Neither then or at any other time had I the slightest intention of being taken prisoner alive.

They turned out to be a patrol from one of the battalions of the Royal Marine Light Infantry in charge of a corporal. Seeing us come from Grandcourt he was quite certain we were a party of Huns. Had we not advanced with our hands up he would have undoubtedly fired on us. Even when we reached him he was not quite sure that we were not Germans disguised, and insisted that we accompany him back to his officer. Fortunately the officer was a fellow I knew who was able to satisfy the corporal that I was all right.

Now that the corporal was placated I guided him and his party back to Grandcourt. We found the Hun position by the simple expedient of walking forward until they opened fire. I then bade the Marines farewell and set out for home. I did not want to go all the way back to the railway lines if I could help it. A short search along the river bank discovered a plank foot-bridge just above the village. Here, I thought, was a stroke of luck and led the way gleefully across it.

We were now on our own side of the river. Seemingly all we had to do was to walk back along the north bank until we once more found our own lines. This we proceeded to do, but had not got very far before we heard voices talking in front of us. In the words of Mr. George Robey, we stopped and we looked and we listened. The voices were talking in German. We were behind the Hun front line.

In the interests of safety I suppose I ought to have turned back and made a detour by way of the railway lines. But I had been out on patrol all night and I was tired. Also, it was getting on for dawn. Besides, I knew there was no wire in front of the Hun line to hold me up. I told my three men to follow me closely and do as I did. Then I crept silently forward.

The voices came closer and closer. At last I could make out the spot where the Huns were congregated. They had no regular trench at this point but were disposed in a series of shell-holes. Nothing could have suited me better. We had passed between two shell-holes before they spotted us. When they eventually challenged we broke into a run.

The Huns were not expecting the enemy to emerge from their rear and were not ready with their rifles. By the time they opened fire, we were half way across No Man's Land. Bullets struck the ground near us but no one was hit. We reached our parapet and jumped down to safety just as the first machine-gun broke into a staccato rattle.

I suppose it was a silly thing to do but none of us was hit and we finished up feeling thoroughly warm, to the envy of our comrades who had remained all night in the trench.

CHAPTER SEVEN

A NIGHT ATTACK

COLONEL BOYLE was delighted with the result of my patrol. Not only had I scored off the Marines, but I had gleaned much valuable information about the Hun position opposite to us. One thing was certain. The Marines could not advance on the other side of the river whilst the enemy held their shell-hole posts on the top of the hill on our side. They could enfilade the whole position with machine-guns and make it untenable. The Colonel announced his intention of visiting Brigade during the day to discuss the matter with the Brigadier. I retired to my dug-out for some sleep.

I took my rest that day in two parts. First I slept until lunch time. I was awake and about during most of the afternoon ; then I went to sleep again after tea. I was awakened about eight-fifteen by my Company Commander shaking me vigorously. He was an Irishman named Sterry Bryan and a great friend of mine, although he had not nearly so great an experience of war as I had. He was one of the fellows given a commission from our reserve battalion, which made him senior to me in commissioned rank though with less than half my active service.

" We've orders to attack, Alf," he informed me as soon as I opened my eyes.

" Splendid ! " I cried, and sat up. " That'll keep

the boys warm at any rate. When is it coming off ? "

"At eleven o'clock to-night," announced Sterry seriously. " It doesn't give us much time, does it ? "

He went on to tell me the reason for the delay. The Coonel spent the afternoon at Brigade making all arrangements. On his way back a shell burst about a quarter of a mile away from him but a flying splinter hit him in the back. He managed to walk the few hundred yards to the Headquarter dug-out, where he collapsed. All he could say was : " I'm hit, Osmond. Get particulars from Brigade about an attack to-night." A second later he was dead. So passed the finest soldier we ever had in the Regiment. He was a man who never knew fear and who inspired all with whom he came in contact with his own enthusiasm.

Ossy hurried at once to Brigade Headquarters where he learned the details of the assault. We were to send two companies over to clear the heights opposite us. A Company were to operate on the right, where the Huns were in shell-hole outposts. B Company were to advance on the left and cut off some three hundred yards of the sunken road. Our left was to rest on a communication trench marked on the map as Miraumont Alley, where a barricade was to be built across the sunken road with sandbags.

Sterry and I carefully discussed the dispositions for B Company. I was to lead the assault with two platoons. Sterry would follow in support with the other two. Every man was to carry a parcel of sandbags and a couple of Mills bombs.

I went down the trench to superintend the distribution of the bombs. Brigade had sent up a supply in boxes for our use. I opened the first box and examined one of the bombs to see it was in order. It was undetonated. A hasty search revealed the fact that none of them was detonated. Someone had blundered.

Had I not been an old bomber they might have been given out and the troops gone into action with weapons as innocuous as tennis balls. I collected some men and we set to work to get them ready for action.

We were ready at last. Five minutes to eleven found the two assaulting platoons lying out in front of the parapet in the snow. The moon was brilliant and it was nearly as light as day.

The barrage opened punctually at eleven o'clock. At once I rose to my feet. In one hand I held my revolver ready for action ; in the other a light walking cane. Billiken reposed in the pocket of my fleece-lined Burberry alongside two Mills bombs. As I walked slowly forward, I glanced to right and left. Dark figures were rising from the ground at intervals of six paces.

Gone were the days when we ran across No Man's Land as fast as we could. The creeping barrage had been introduced and an attack was now a scientific performance worked out to a time-table. We had nine minutes in which to cover four hundred yards. We could take our time and preserve a perfect line.

The shells were whistling overhead and bursting in front of us in a long irregular line. After the first three minutes the barrage lifted to just in front of the sunken road. We followed. We were right up to it within fifty yards of our objective with three minutes to spare. I knelt down on one knee and concentrated on my watch. Six minutes past eleven ; seven minutes past eleven. I still looked hard, but the minute hand refused to move any further. With a shock of dismay I realised it had stopped. No doubt the concussions of the barrage were too much for it.

What should I do ? Unless I was on the Hun parapet when the barrage finally lifted Fritz might have time to offer us a stubborn resistance. I rose to my feet and moved rapidly forward.

Thinking it over afterwards I believe I must have started down the slope of the sunken road about thirty seconds before the barrage jumped. One moment shells seemed to be bursting all around me ; the next they were fifty yards ahead and I was all alone. At least I thought I was all alone. No one appeared to have followed me ; no enemy appeared to oppose me. Then all at once I saw two long flashes of light immediately in front of me. My eyes focussed on two Huns about ten yards away who had fired their rifles at me. In the excitement of the moment they both missed. I took careful aim and fired. One man collapsed in a heap. The other clapped his hands to his body and screamed wildly. I fired another shot. He pitched forward on his face.

By now the road was full of our men. Sergeant Snoad was at my elbow calm and collected. We must find Miraumont Alley. With Snoad and half a dozen men at my heels, I ran forward along the road. Huns barred our passage. One instant they were there ; the next they were swept away. I fired my revolver ; Snoad got one with his bayonet ; the men were shooting and stabbing.

I fired again and again. There was no resistance to my pull on the trigger. My magazine was empty. I must reload. I broke open my pistol and pulled out a handful of cartridges. I was so intent on reloading that I failed to notice a shell-hole in front of me. My foot stepped on air. I pitched forward on my face.

The men behind thought I was hit, and, deprived of my leadership, formed a line and commenced firing over my prostrate figure. I was in the deuce of a position. I dare not sit up or I should have got one of our bullets through my head. I turned over on my back and started to shout.

Snoad was the first to realise I was unhurt. At once he stopped the men firing. I got to my feet.

" Bring a Lewis gun ! " I ordered.

The moment the Lewis gun opened fire down the road resistance ceased. The rattle of a machine-gun has a marvellous moral effect. We found the opening into Miraumont Alley without difficulty. Snoad found the platoon who had been detailed to build the barricade and set them to work whilst I went down the road to organise the position ready for the counter-attack which I expected almost immediately. I knew Fritz's methods. He always counter-attacked as soon as possible with whatever troops he could collect, trusting to the value of surprise to help him regain the lost position. If he failed he prepared a rather more elaborate assault which was launched about two hours later.

I found the men in splendid fettle. Everybody was in his allotted place and all were prepared. I gave an eye to the Lewis gun positions to make sure the guns had a good field of fire. There were two German machine-guns in the trench which we had captured. Some of our machine-gunners understood how they worked so we rigged them up in our defence. They materially increased our armament.

Sterry came along whilst I was seeing to this. He had been down the other end of the road to get in touch with A Company attacking on our right. They had taken the shell-hole positions without any difficulty and were engaged in strengthening the position. We went along together to have a look at the barricade. Snoad had the situation well in hand and the sandbag wall was mounting rapidly.

" I wonder what's happened to D Company ? " said Sterry. D Company should have filled the gap which we had made between our old position and our new by coming forward. All they had to do was to extend along the old German communication trench Miraumont Alley until they connected with us. For some reason the Company Commander had misunderstood his orders and had failed to move.

Sterry decided to go back and see what had happened to them and started off down Miraumont Alley with only his runner behind him. Scarcely had he started than the barrage commenced for the Hun counter-attack. Beyond that I expected him back any minute all thoughts of Sterry passed out of my mind. All my energies were concentrated on seeing that the Hun counter-attack was a failure. I moved from man to man and from gun to gun. Everyone was at his post and on the alert.

Suddenly someone cried, "They're coming!"

I stood on the parapet and peered into the night. A long line of dark figures was moving rapidly towards us. Somewhere on my right a machine-gun broke into song. Another took up the chorus. Rifles joined in with their individual notes. But still the dark line came forward.

I despatched my runner to the spot we had appointed as temporary Company H.Q. The sergeant-major was waiting for my order. He had a fuse ready in his hand. The moment my runner arrived with the word for which he had been waiting he lit the three rockets which were ready in their sockets.

Red, green, red; they soared one after the other into the sky. It was the S.O.S. for our artillery support and had a similar effect to turning on a tap. Almost before the third rocket had tailed away into nothingness, our call was answered. Swish! Swish! Swish! Bang! Bang! Bang! Crack! Crack! Crack! Shrapnel and high explosive came flying to our aid. The long dark line halted, wavered, and was swept away before that irresistible tornado of shells and bullets. The firs counter-attack was over. We were safe—at least, so I thought. Someone caught me roughly by the arm.

I turned quickly. Sterry Bryan's runner was behind

me, white-faced and frightened. He was breathing hard as though he had been running. He pointed his finger towards Miraumont Alley.

"We're surrounded, sir," he cried. "The Huns are behind us. They've killed Captain Bryan!"

This was indeed startling news. My first thought was for the safety of the trench. I called Sergeant Burgess who was a few paces from me, and rapidly explained the position.

"Take every third man and guard the parados," I ordered. "You take charge of them and see they don't fire unless they're absolutely certain they're aiming at Huns. I'm going down to see what's happened."

I collected half a dozen bombs and a sergeant named Sly and together with my runner hurried along to Miraumont Alley. As I approached the entrance to the trench I could see what remarkable progress they were making with the barricade. It was now almost the height of a man and thick enough to stop almost anything. It would not be long before it was completed.

Once in Miraumont Alley I proceeded with the greatest caution. I had not gone more than a hundred yards when a voice shouted something in German. Almost at the same moment I heard the soft whistle of a burning fuse and a bomb passed over my head and burst behind me. At once I saw my advantage, and dropping on my hands and knees I motioned my two followers to do likewise. We crept quietly forward for another ten yards and then halted. Bomb after bomb went hurtling by to burst further down the trench. Not knowing where we were the Huns were throwing their bombs as far as they could. It was the natural thing for them to do when surprised at night.

I waited for some quarter of an hour without moving. By that time I judged that they would have concluded that we had withdrawn. Then the three of us heaved over three bombs apiece as fast as we could. The effect was instantaneous. We got a couple of them and the rest fled. They had been taken completely by surprise.

I sent Sergeant Sly down to bring up D Company to connect and then returned to the sunken road. Soon afterwards D Company arrived headed by Bill Finch and his platoon. I asked him to send out a patrol to make sure there were no more Huns in rear of us. Then, with a relieved mind I turned my attention once more to consolidating the position.

I was now the only officer left in the Company. In addition to Sterry two subalterns had been wounded by shell-fire and gone down. Burgess and Snoad were quite as good as any officers I could have had. With their assistance I knew I should pull through. Just now all my attention was concentrated on preparing for the big counter-attack which I knew would be launched very shortly.

One of our Lewis guns was out of action. So was one of the German machine-guns which I had brought into use. A five point nine had made a direct hit on it and it was no more. I examined the rest of our armament and made sure that the machine-gunners had plenty of ammunition handy. All the men were quite cheery and I had no misgivings about them making a good show when the time came.

We had not very long to wait. The Hun put down a barrage ten times as great in intensity as before. It was a taste of what we might expect. Of course they had the range to an inch and a sunken road is a devilishly exposed place to be in during a bombardment. I waited as before until the attack had actually started before I sent up the S.O.S. for the artillery. Again I sent my runner down to Company H.Q. with a message. Every second I expected the rockets to go up. Nothing happened. The Huns were coming steadily forward.

I left the parapet and ran down to find out the cause of the delay.

It was the simplest of human troubles. The sergeant-major could not get a match to light in the wind. My runner tried, I tried, we all tried. At last we got one red rocket to start. The others simply would not light. We kept on trying until we had exhausted all our matches and then gave it up. Fortunately someone was watching at Battalion H.Q., and coupling the single rocket with the noise of the fight, had the sense to 'phone through for artillery support.

With the welcome sound of our counter-barrage in my ears I set out for the parapet. The Huns—what were left of them—were now within a hundred yards. I wondered whether it was coming to a hand-to-hand scrap. Something hit me in the centre of my forehead and I went down like a log. For a moment I lay stunned, stars floated before my eyes. Then I picked myself up and recovered my steel helmet. There was a dent in the centre of it the size of an orange.

I was feeling deadly faint, but somebody told me the Huns were running. I think that helped to revive me. I went back into the road. A shell burst just behind me and a splinter hit me on the back of the head making a second dent, though not such a big one as the first. I had scarcely replaced my hat for the second time when something sharp pierced my back just below the shoulder blade. The air was raining shells.

Snoad came along and dragged me to the side of the road. I was still too dazed to think clearly and was standing in the most exposed spot in the road. Men were falling like ninepins. I could have wept with the maddening impotence of my position. We had come over the top with one hundred and fifty men and four officers. I was now the only officer left, and I was wounded slightly, and I had about sixty men.

Would they attack again at dawn? That was the

leading question. I waited until their artillery had slackened down and then once again made a tour of the position. The men mere marvellous considering the ordeal they had been through. Down on the right, where the Miraumont-Beaucourt road ran through our trench, there was an endless procession of stretchers taking away the wounded. We could not possibly evacuate all the cases before the morning. Only the worst ones could be dealt with. We should have to make the rest of them as comfortable as possible until the next night.

At last came the dawn. We stood to and waited, grimy and weary, but no attack materialised. Fritz had had enough of us. The sunken road at Baillescourt Farm was ours.

I crept into a dug-out which Fritz had started in the parados. Someone put some iodine and a field-dressing on the slight wound in my back made by the shrapnel. My servant supplied a hot drink with a large sized tot of rum in it. I lay me down. Almost before my head touched the ground I was asleep.

CHAPTER EIGHT

BAILLESCOURT FARM

THE following is a copy of a letter I wrote home on the 16th February :

DEAREST MATER,

I expect you have wondered why the devil I have got slack in writing again. As a matter of fact I have been unable to. The battalion have had about the hardest time they have ever had while I have been with them. It was quite impossible to get letters away.

We went into the line for a couple of days with the ground frozen hard and sat and shivered. I had a difficult reconnaissance to do which was fortunately successful. I will tell you more about that when I come home again. The result of my report was that we went over the top the next night to capture the trench in front. There was practically no resistance on our right, but, on the left flank, where I happened to be in command, they tried to stop us. I was the first man over the Hun parapet and landed right on top of two Huns who tried to do me in, but fortunately I managed to finish them off with my jolly old revolver. Hand-to-hand fighting was rather fun but we soon cleared them out.

The only man senior to me got killed leaving me in command. I discovered a party of Huns behind me at one time but settled their hash after about two hours, and settled down.

We held the trench for several days during which time Fritz tried to shell us out again. I got hit three times, but only slightly, so I stayed where I was. I had my steel helmet dented in at the front to a hole as big as a fair sized egg and then I had it smashed in at the back, and finally I got hit just below the shoulder blade in the back. The effect of all this only lasted about forty-eight hours and now I am quite fit again with the exception of recurrent headaches.

Now we are out again resting, covered in glory. The Brigadier very kindly informed me that he has recommended me for a medal, so you will probably see me down for an M.C. in the next list of honours. I am also in charge of a Company, so am having a busy time.

I leave it to you to prevent the Pater from having this copied or put in any newspaper, and am simply telling you for your own personal information.

I want some thick socks also a new torch (Ever ready) to fit the refills I still have.

Heaps of love.

The M.C. materialised in due course. The official notice in the *Gazette* ran as follows :

" Second Lieutenant Alfred Oliver Pollard, Honourable Artillery Company, has been awarded the Military Cross, for gallantry and devotion to duty in the field. Lieutenant Pollard led a patrol and carried out a dangerous reconnaissance. Later, he assumed command of a Company and repulsed two strong enemy counter-attacks."

Fritz made no further attempt on the sunken road after the first night. I think he must have suffered pretty heavily in his two counter-attacks to judge by the number of corpses strewn about No Man's Land. Instead he concentrated on shelling us out. Day after day he plastered us at intervals of every few hours. Try what I would my casualty list slowly mounted.

There was only one proper dug-out in the road ; a huge one capable of holding forty men. It had two entrances. They had sunk the shaft for a third, or possibly an extension of the dug-out. It was this shaft that I selected as Company H.Q., leaving the big dug-out for the men. When the periodical shelling started I withdrew all the men from the trench with the exception of a handful of sentries and mustered them in the dug-out. It was rather a risk as there was always the possibility of an attack following the barrage. Everyone stood ready with his equipment on and his rifle in his hand, prepared to dash out to his firing position. We tried it once or twice as a drill and concluded that it was worth while both from the point of conservation of life and the equally important one of keeping up the *moral*.

Moral is always a difficult question at the best of times. The deadly monotony of sitting about all day doing nothing wears down the keenest nerves. Normally it is up to the Officer in command to arrange easy spells of digging and trench improvement to occupy his men's minds. But during this trip the snow lay thick on the ground and the frost was so deep that it was next to impossible to use a pick. Had it been summer I should have moved forward a hundred yards and dug a fresh trench. As it was I was deterred by the difficulty of digging and the fact that the big dug-out provided some shelter where the men could get some sleep in comfort during their turn off duty.

Things seemed fairly quiet on the second night so I left the trench in charge of Snoad and Burgess and went down to see Ossy. I also wanted to get my wound treated by the Doctor. It made a very cheerful break to sit for an hour at Headquarters and have a chat with Ossy. He insisted on talking of every subject under the sun except my sunken road. He said it would give my mind a rest and it certainly did. I went back to my job feeling very cheery.

Ossy sent me a platoon from C Company to strengthen my garrison. The one chosen was that commanded by " Ox " Holder. I was delighted to have him but, like myself, he is a six-footer and took up a tremendous amount of room in our tiny dug-out. There was a sort of shelf where we used to park him when we wanted to have a meal. He gave me a great deal of help though and took a lot of responsibility off my shoulders.

Dawn was always the time when things happened. Every morning provided some fresh excitement. Usually one or more Huns came over to give themselves up. The first time there were two of them, both men of over fifty. Neither could speak English and none of us could speak German so we had to resort to signs. From what I could make out they tried to tell us that they were very cold and very hungry. They certainly looked very miserable.

Another day it was a youngster. He was very much more perky and could speak English. He started off by asking for a cigarette. Someone gave him one. Then he wanted a match. That was a fairly natural request so someone fixed him up with a light. He puffed contentedly for a few moments and then asked calmly whether he might be sent to the same internment camp in England as his cousin.

Then, one evening, a poet made an attempt. He may have been able to write poetry but he was a fool at the same time. He came walking fast down the Miraumont-Beaucourt road just after dusk. We had a road post with a Lewis gun. The sentry heard him coming and challenged, " Halt ! " Instead of complying the poet broke into a run. The sentry challenged again but the poet still came on. Thinking he might be intending to run up and throw a bomb the sentry fired a short burst

190

from the Lewis gun. The poet fell dead within ten yards of his objective. We found his book of poetry in his pocket. The last poem, dedicated to his mother, was unfinished. It told how he intended to give himself up to the English because he was so cold. Poor devil! If he had had the sense to walk instead of run he would probably be alive to this day.

Another night a man did walk down that road. He was adorned with his full equipment, his rifle was slung over his shoulder, and he was singing softly to himself. The guard withheld their fire because of his unsteady gait. He was lurching from side to side of the road. They seized him as he reached the road post. He was dead drunk and thoroughly amazed to find himself a prisoner. He was returning to his unit after leave and had lost his way.

But the creamiest of all these little incidents was on the fifth morning. There was a slight mist which made it rather difficult to see more than a few yards. We were consequently rather more vigilant than usual. Suddenly Lance-Corporal Freter hopped over the parapet and ran forward with his rifle at the ready. A few minutes later he reappeared through the mist driving two Huns before him. One was a Prussian lieutenant and the other was a sergeant-major. Both were very surly. We sent them down to Headquarters where Ossy questioned them. It turned out that each was in command of a Company; the Officer's Company was relieving the sergeant-major's Company. They had lost their way in the fog whilst going round the posts. Both Companies of men were waiting for them in the trench. What a delicious situation. I have often wondered how long they waited before someone tumbled to what had happened to their leaders.

Despite the cold, despite the shelling and the casualties, we had a lot of fun in that trench. It's an ill wind that blows nobody any good. Army regulations provide that rations must be indented for three days ahead. Consequently three days after the attack we were still receiving the full rations for one hundred and fifty men. And there were less than fifty men to share them. That was all very nice with the food but it was a different question with the rum. I made an issue twice a day but I still had a lot over. I dare not issue any more because it has a very potent effect in exceptionally cold weather. I did not want to make my tiny garrison tight.

The only thing we were rather short of was water. All water had to be carried up to us in petrol tins and, in spite of the extra rations, there was barely enough for the extra hot gripes necessary to keep out the cold. The men melted snow and boiled it. It was against regulations but I closed my eyes to it. One must relax somewhere.

We were all right. We discovered a supply of Hun soda water in our dug-out and an enterprising servant boiled it and made tea. It was not too bad when mixed with rum to take away the taste. I hardly recommend it though except perhaps to try once.

We were relieved on the seventh night. My Company had now dwindled to thirty-five but all were of good heart. We marched back to the transport field without a single man falling out. The Brigadier rode out part way to meet us and thanked the men for the fine show they had put up. I thought it rather decent of him.

We were all thoroughly tired and in need of a rest. I for one was jolly glad to turn in and fall asleep knowing I was free from sudden alarms necessitating a dash out into the trench. It was also a great relief to get my clothes off again and turn in between blankets. There is one thing I will say for war. It makes one appreciate the blessedness of sleep.

CHAPTER NINE

BEAUREGARD DOVECOTE

OUR rest only lasted a few days. We were back in the line again within a week. This time in support. My Company were posted in deep dug-outs cut out of the chalk. They were nice and dry. We were very lucky to have them. Outside in the trench, the water was knee deep. There had been a thaw and it was impossible to walk a yard without slipping.

One night one of my sentries reported that he had found a straggler wandering about utterly exhausted. He was a Company sergeant-major of Marines and he had lost his way. I had him brought down into my dug-out to revive him a bit before we sent him back. After some hot food and a tot of rum he gave us his opinion of trench warfare.

" Give me the bleeding North Sea every time," he said tersely. " That's where I spent last winter and it was a picnic compared with this. Even if it was a bit cold on watch it was nice and warm when you turned in below. Here, you stands up to your waist in water while you're on duty. Then, when you're relieved, you go down into a blinkin' deep dug-out like some blasted rabbit, and the rain comes pouring down the stairs after you and you has to sleep in a puddle of water. You can't get away from it."

We roared with laughter. There is a sort of grim satisfaction in knowing that you are undergoing greater hardships than the other fellow. It gives one a glow of inward righteousness. Not that I think the Infantry had the worst time of any unit in the War by any means. I give that unenviable distinction to the gunners serving eighteen-pounders. The Infantryman only had himself to look after; the gunner had his horses. Infantry in the front lines could only be shelled by the lighter guns because of the big margin of error of the big stuff. The gunners got everything; during an action they were subjected to continuous bombardment from the heaviest calibred guns the enemy possessed. Although everybody will not agree with me, the Infantryman had the fun of going over the top and the chance of getting some of his own back in a hand to hand contest. The gunner never saw the effect of his shells, nor even whether he had hit anything at all.

We were not left very long in the peace and quiet of support. One night Colonel Osmond sent me orders to attend a conference of Company Commanders. The news was extremely exhilarating. Fritz was believed to be retiring. We were to follow him up on the following morning. Companies would move independently in artillery formation. Our objective was a ruined farm on a hill-top called Beauregard Dovecote. If the enemy were still there we were to clear him out. When we had occupied the position we were to dispose ourselves with one Company in front and the others in support and reserve.

"I'm giving you the post of honour, Alfred," smiled Charlie Osmond. "Your Company did so well in the last show that it's only right that you should be in the vanguard now."

That was always Ossy's attitude. To him honour was more than life. The tradition of the Regiment meant everything.

We formed up just in front of my old sunken road shortly after dawn. It was our very first experience of open warfare since the battalion crossed to France in 1914. Everyone was very excited. If the Hun was going back did this mean the end of the War ? If so we would give him a push which would hasten things.

Two minutes before zero hour I fell in a shell-hole. I was standing examining my map, and was too engrossed to notice that my foot was sinking in the mud. When I went to move my foot stuck and jerked me over backwards. There was a shell-hole immediately behind me and I sat down in it. Unfortunately it was full of water and I got soaked to the skin. Somebody helped me up. A moment later we got the word to move and I forgot all about it.

At that time of the morning the ground was covered by a light mist which was fortunate for us in that it cloaked our movements. At the same time it was extremely difficult to find our way over strange ground without being able to pick up any landmarks. Our objective was about a mile in front of us and we had an anxious time making it. We had covered nearly half the distance when I suddenly made out a body of men crossing our path at right angles. For a moment I thought they were Huns and was on the point of giving the order to extend when my runner called out that they were D Company. Now it was obvious that we could not both be going in the right direction. One of us was hopelessly wrong. The question was which ?

I went across and had a few words with the officer in charge of D Company. He was positive he was right. So was I. So we both went our way. He was using a compass. I was following the contours of the ground marked on the map. I had had some experience before of the deflections which barbed wire can cause in a compass. Ten minutes later one of my scouts came running back to report that he had walked dead on to the farm and it was unoccupied.

I carefully disposed my men in a line of shell-holes

by the side of the road which ran in front of the farm and began a tour of inspection. The first thing I noticed was that the country was covered in grass. With the exception of a few shell-holes dotted here and there the ground was unspoiled. It was a wonderful feeling, after three years of War to think we had burst our way right through the devastated area. It made one really believe we had Fritz on the run. The end of the struggle seemed almost in sight. It was very heartening.

I had sent a messenger to Headquarters the moment I arrived to say I was in position. A chit came back to say I was to extend my front to the outskirts of Miraumont. I was also to patrol the road as far as the top of the ridge overlooking Puisieux. It meant that I was responsible for something over one thousand yards of front and I had thirty-five men with which to do it. I should not have had as many as that if my Company had not been endowed with most wonderful grit. The day before I had eight sick men marked medicine and duty which meant that they need not have gone into action unless they wished. I put it to them and they all volunteered to accompany me. All got across to the farm except one who fainted on the way from the weight of his equipment.

I disposed them in pairs in convenient shell-holes from fifty to one hundred yards apart. We should have been absolutely useless against any organised attack but we were in a position to repel any raid or minor offensive. As I passed the farm I ran into a unit of the Machine-Gun Corps who had come too far forward in the mist. It was commanded by a young subaltern just out from England who did not know the ropes very well. The thing that interested me was that he had four Vickers guns each with a team of experienced men. I speedily took him under my wing and disposed his guns on the hill-top round the farm in such a way that my Company had adequate protection should they need it. They were equivalent to a reinforcement of one hundred men. That done I felt quite safe.

The mist cleared off about eleven o'clock and we were able to see what was opposite. From the road where we were in position the ground sloped down into a valley which rose again to the crest of a ridge about seven hundred yards in front of us. According to the map Fritz had a trench running along the ridge called Gudgeon trench. He soon showed us it was occupied by firing some bursts from machine-guns placed to cross one another's fire and enfilade the valley. At once I realised the game we should have had getting into position had not the mist befriended us. As it was we were nice and snug.

We waited all day in imminent expectation of orders to take the ridge in front but nothing happened. Sitting still, I gradually became more and more conscious of the fact that I was soaked through. During the day it was not so bad, but night brought a sharp spring frost. I felt chilled and miserable, unable to stay in one place for more than a few minutes. I spent most of the night walking up and down the road trying to keep warm.

Being the only officer in the Company I was unable to leave my men. Other fellows from other Companies visited me however and helped me pass the night. From one visitor I learned that D Company did not reach their position in support until the afternoon.

Dawn came and still no orders to move. It seemed madness to delay when we had a chance to harry Fritz in his retirement. The reason was furnished in the afternoon. We were to be relieved by a fresh Division new out from England and consequently up to full strength.

I was bitterly disappointed. With Fritz retiring and the end of the War in sight we were not to be allowed to participate. It was too bad that a new Division was to have the honour of finishing what we had started. However, orders are orders and have to be obeyed. An hour after dusk the Company of the new Division who were to relieve me arrived to take over. They were a Yorkshire battalion in the 65th Division. The Company Commander asked me how many men I had for him to replace.

" Thirty-five," I replied.

" Good Heavens ! " he exclaimed. " I shall never be able to get all mine in. I've two hundred and fifty ! "

" Never mind," I consoled him. " You've twelve hundred yards for them to spread out in."

The poor devil looked at me in blank astonishment. All he had learned about warfare at his school of instruction had gone by the board in his first minute of experience. Nobody had ever suggested to him that thirty-five men might hold twelve hundred yards of front.

We marched back that night to the transport field. All the way down we passed gun-teams toiling to get their guns forward to new positions in pursuit of the enemy. Cursing men and sweating horses ; a wheel embedded in the mud at the bottom of a shell-hole. Poor devils of gunners. How lucky we were to be in the Infantry.

This time we went right out for a rest. We were billeted in Nissen huts and were quite comfortable. Once more the Spring made us a promise of warmer weather. The sun was brilliant and we were able to go about without overcoats.

We lazed about until nearly the end of March. Then one day we received orders that the Division was to move South. The night before we were due to start I sprained my ankle by falling into a trench in the dark. The following morning the battalion moved off leaving me alone on my bed, the sole occupant of the camp.

CHAPTER TEN

GAVRELLE

I SENT the following letter to my mother on the 25th April, 1917 :

DEAREST LADYBIRD,

Here we are again, out once more. I have had some most interesting and exciting times since last writing, including going over the top again. I am once more in charge of the Company as the man senior to me got laid out with a bullet. I shall probably be a Captain again in a day or two, but one never knows as somebody else senior may be sent along. You see the present arrangement of the government is that all promotions are by seniority irrespective of fighting qualities, so really one has no chance of being more than a Second Lieutenant whatever one does. However, I don't care a bit what rank I am.

I had a most exciting adventure in a Hun trench the other day. I cut through their wire and got into their trench thinking it was unoccupied, but soon discovered it was full of Huns and consequently had to beat a hasty retreat. I got out all right fortunately. I hear a rumour that the Brigadier has recommended me for a bar to my M.C. in consequence of this little business so if you keep your eyes glued on the paper you may shortly see my name in it. Don't think I have been taking any unnecessary risks because I have not. I have merely done what I have been asked to do.

Well, dear old lady, although out of the line we are still away from civilization. By the way I have received another box of new records but cannot play the wretched gramophone until those governor springs arrive so please hurry them up.

Best of spirits and having a good time. By the way, I have killed another Hun. Hurrah!

Well, cheerioh!

I have included this letter because it throws such a clear light on my attitude towards war at this time. I thoroughly enjoyed going into action and was never happier than when there was something doing. People tell me I must have a kink in my nature; that my zest to be in the forefront of the battle was unnatural. I do not agree with them. I have often thought about it since the War and the conclusion I have reached is that my condition of mind was simply a keen desire to win. I wanted the British to be victorious and was prepared to strain every nerve to attain that end. True, I wanted to be in at the death myself, but I think that was a natural rather than an unnatural wish. At this time also, I was convinced that it only needed a little extra effort for us to break through the Germans' last line of defence. I was bitterly disappointed when we failed to do so.

When the battalion marched away and left me lying alone in my hut, the doctor had made arrangements for me to be conveyed to the nearest Casualty Clearing Station. Once again I hoped to be able to persuade them to let me rest a few days until my ankle was better so that I might rejoin my unit as speedily as possible. Once again the hospital authorities defeated me. They had a certain routine and they refused to depart from it by one jot or tittle.

Down to the Base I went, my mind a seething fury. This time it was No 8 General Hospital, Rouen, where all were strangers and I had no friendly Sister to make my stay enjoyable. I was able to hobble about after eight days in bed. After a fortnight I was discharged and sent to that wretched camp at Havre where I was before. My friend the Adjutant, mindful of the second ribbon which adorned my tunic, was considerably more friendly and respectful. I ventured to suggest he should use his influence to get me sent up the line again as soon as possible. He was vastly astonished that anyone should want to hasten back to the trenches when he had a chance of miking at the Base, but he consented to do what he could. I was in a fever of impatience. I had heard that the battalion were still out resting but I knew that this state of affairs could not last much longer.

The 9th of April arrived. In due course we heard of the brilliant storming of the Vimy Ridge by the 51st and the Canadian Divisions. The Naval Division were in the neighbourhood. I felt sure they would soon be in it. On the 10th I received my movement orders. There were only nineteen of the H.A.C. in the Camp. I was to take them with me. Seventeen of them were fresh from England; of the two others, one was a corporal whom I put in charge of the draft, the other was a private who temporarily acted as my servant.

We got away on a train that night. The following night we were at Abbeville shunted on to a siding in that enormous railway clearing yard. By the luck of the devil I found one of the R.T.O.'s, who was an O.M.T.; Artie Barrett, a younger brother of H. Roper Barrett. He found out the exact location of the battalion for me and had my draft put on a train at the earliest possible moment. We reached a station—I have forgotten the name—at five o'clock on the evening of the 12th. I knew we were somewhere near our destination and hopped out to interview the R.T.O. He told me that the train would not be going near the Regiment but that there was another one in the opposite platform that was. I gave hurried orders to the draft to make the change. There was only a minute or so for them to get their kit together and the new fellows were not quick enough in the up-take. When I finally arrived at my terminus the only people besides myself who got out of the train were the corporal and my temporary servant. The draft had disappeared.

We walked a couple of miles and rejoined the battalion. I reported to the Orderly Room at seven o'clock.

" Well played, Alf ! " cried Charlie Osmond. " You're in the nick of time. We're leaving on motor buses at six to-morrow morning to follow up the attack on the Vimy Ridge."

My heart leapt within me. I had made it. Nobody would have the opportunity of calling me a coward this time.

The Adjutant looked up from some papers he was consulting on his desk.

" I was advised that you were bringing a draft," he remarked. " Where are they ? "

" I've lost them," I said innocently.

The Adjutant was horrified. He had the official mind which believes that orders should be carried out to the letter and not merely in the spirit. I laughed. What did I care about the draft now that I was back with my beloved battalion. The wretched draft eventually reported some six weeks later after having caused consternation to half the R.T.O.'s and Town Majors in France. Nobody seemed to know what to do with a draft who did not appear to be anybody's responsibility.

Of course I had been deposed from the command of B Company. George Thorpe had been transferred from A, and as he happened to be senior to me I was obliged to take second place. However I got on very well with old George and I felt quite sure we should pull together which was the great thing.

The following morning the buses took us up to the line. We disembarked on the eastern side of Arras and marched to a line of captured trenches in support, known as the Black line. Various objectives had been designated by the Staff, Black line, Red line, Green line, etc., for easy reference. After two days in support we moved forward to the village of Bailleul, which was the British front line.

Here we were still over a mile from the Bosche who was believed to have fallen back to a strongly entrenched position in the next valley known as the Hindenburg Line. On the afternoon of the 16th, a Brigade Major carefully examined this trench system through his binoculars, and, failing to observe any signs of life, came to the conclusion that Fritz must have fallen back even further. He at once issued orders that patrols were to be sent out at intervals of five hundred yards by all units in the front line. Each patrol was to consist of an officer and twelve men. The orders were that they were to proceed to the Hindenburg Line and, if they found it unoccupied, take possession of it and send word back for their respective battalions to move forward and join them.

My battalion furnished two patrols of which I was ordered to take one. I at once asked whether I might be permitted to amend my instructions and take only four men. I was used to patrolling at night with four men and I considered a party of twelve too unwieldy to control in the darkness. I was overruled, however, and it was with a corporal and eleven men that I set out shortly after nightfall.

There was no moon. The night was pitch black and the rain was coming down in a slight drizzle. It was extremely difficult to see more than ten yards ahead.

The Hun artillery was searching and sweeping which meant that odd shells were falling here, there and everywhere in the blind hope of hitting something. I was far too much of a fatalist at this period of the War for them to affect me, but several of my patrol were young soldiers and the haphazard shelling had a considerable effect on their nerves. I had not gone very far before I began to seriously think of dumping two-thirds of them in a shell-hole and picking them up on my return. Many times since I have wished to goodness that I had but at the time I carried on with them.

It was fairly easy going for the first half mile. We were following the railway line from Arras to Gavrelle, and all we had to do was to walk alongside the sleepers. I had made a thorough study of the map and had memorised all the salient features so that I had very little fear of failing to find my way.

Just short of the crest of the ridge the railway made a sharp turn to the south. This was the spot at which I had decided to leave it and strike across country. Two or three hundred yards to the north was a small clump of trees, which, standing on the crest of the ridge, gave me a landmark from which to take my bearings. At least I had intended to use it for that purpose had the night been sufficiently light for me to see it at a distance. As it was I had to search about until I found it.

We were now about four hundred yards from the Hun position which stretched along the bottom of the valley. Standing facing it, Oppy Wood was about forty-five degrees to my left hand whilst Gavrelle town was about the same angle to the right. Even though I could not see I knew I could not very well lose my way with these well-defined boundaries to limit my wanderings.

Followed by my patrol, I moved slowly forward down the slope. The Hun position was invisible in the inky blackness. Evidently they were not expecting any visitors, for there was a complete absence of star-shells. I began to wonder whether the Brigade Major might not be right in his assumption that Fritz had withdrawn further than was expected. We should soon know. All the same I decided to take all possible precautions.

Half way down from the ridge I came across a hole in the ground which had been dug for some purpose and abandoned. Here I posted two of my men with instructions that if they heard a shindy in front and a lot of firing, and none of us came back, they were to return to Headquarters with the news of what had happened.

Two hundred yards further on we encountered the first row of German barbed wire entanglements. It was a very thick obstacle and we had some difficulty in getting through it. We made a lot of noise cutting our way, so much that I felt sure we should have been heard were the trench occupied. A few yards further on was another line of wire as difficult to negotiate as the first. We broke through this without any attempt to keep quiet as it seemed impossible that any of the enemy were in the vicinity. I left a man posted by the gap we had made in each belt of wire to facilitate our return.

We were now on the parapet of the trench. Feeling with the cane which I carried in my hand I felt my way to the edge. What should I do next ? My orders were to occupy the position and send back for the rest of the battalion. Had I better do so or should I proceed a bit further and try and locate the Huns' exact situation ? Was I absolutely certain that the trench before me was completely unoccupied ?

The question in my mind was answered by the flash from a Very pistol some two or three hundred yards to my right. Someone was in the trench at any rate. Standing quite still from force of habit, I watched the light describe its parabola in the sky. It cast a shadow at my feet and I idly poked my cane at it. To my surprise my cane went through the shadow and revealed a crack of light.

My heart leapt in a sudden acceleration of beats. This was very, very interesting. I dropped on to my hands and knees and bent my ear to the crack. I could hear voices talking in German; there was an occasional burst of laughter. We were standing over the entrance to a Hun dug-out.

I got hastily to my feet. If there was one dug-out there would be others. The Huns were apparently sheltering from the rain which was now coming down fairly fast. All the same there would be some sentries in the trench somewhere. Either they were shirking their work or one would pass this way very shortly.

My first thought was for my men. With that barbed wire between us and our reinforcements it would be madness for me to think of occupying a position of that strength with a dozen men. I must get them back through the wire before I decided what I would do.

I gave whispered instructions to retire. Corporal Larsen backed me up magnificently, but some of the inexperienced ones were inclined to panic a bit and they made enough noise getting through that belt of wire to wake the dead. All the same we got through both that belt and the next one without raising the alarm. Then we counted them to make sure they were all there. One was missing. Allowing for the two I had posted in a hole in the ground, there were only nine where there should have been ten. Where could he be? What the blazes should I do? There was only one thing for it. I must look for him.

I gave Larsen instructions to take the rest of the patrol back to the clump of trees and wait for me behind the shelter of the ridge. Then my runner, Reggie Hughesdon, and I climbed back through the wire. Our

206

man was nowhere between the first and second belts so we went on to the parapet. I thought the missing one might be the man I had left in charge of one of the gaps.

I emerged from the second line of barbed wire and turned to help Reggie. Someone challenged me sharply from the trench. I spun round in time to see the flash of his rifle. I fired two shots and heard him yell as I hit him.

The firing gave the alarm. Men were appearing in the trench like magic. Reggie and I were caught like rats in a trap. It would have been impossible to have broken our way out through the wire without offering a sitting target to the enemy.

There was only one thing to do. I seized Reggie by the arm and ran. Down the parapet we flew as fast as our legs would take us. Star-shells were going up in all directions. By their light I could see that the trench was of a pattern known as island traversed. That meant that there were two trenches parallel with one another joined at short intervals by cross-cuts. At intervals along the parapet were squares of concrete which I knew to be machine-gun emplacements. I realised it was a position that would take a lot of capturing.

We must have covered well over a hundred yards before I spotted it. It was a miracle that I saw it at all—just a narrow gap in the wire entanglement left so that the holders of the trench could get out easily if they wished to. I darted into it with Reggie close on my heels. It zig-zagged through both lines of wire. In a moment we were free of our cage.

Down on our hands and knees behind the shelter of the wire. We had scarcely dropped before rifles and machine-guns opened up behind us. I prayed that Larsen had got the patrol safely over the top of the ridge. Reggie and I were as safe as if we were out of range. No bullets could pierce that doubly thick screen of wire which protected us from our assailants.

We were safe from bullets but there was another menace which threatened us. I guessed it would be only a question of minutes before Fritz organised a patrol to look for us. We must get clear of his gateway. We crawled along behind our cover in the direction from which we had come. Five minutes later a sudden cessation of fire warned me they were coming. Reggie and I sank motionless to the ground whilst a long line of dark figures dashed out through the zig-zag path. There must have been at least twenty of them. If they had searched along the front of the wire they would have found us, but I had banked on that being the one place they would overlook.

We stayed where we were for half an hour until the Huns had returned to their trench and all the excitement had died away. Then we rejoined Larsen on the ridge and made a startling discovery. In the rush of getting the patrol back into safety he had neglected to pick up the two men I had posted in the hole in the ground. Reggie and I went down to look for them but they had disappeared. We sent the patrol home and continued our search until daylight. No trace could be found of them. We learned afterwards that the Hun patrol had run into them, killing one and taking the other prisoner.

They gave me a bar to my Military Cross for that show. I do not know what sort of a report went in; the *Official Gazette* read as follows:

"Sec. Lt. Alfred Oliver Pollard, M.C., H.A.C.—He carried out a dangerous reconnaissance of the enemy's front line under very heavy fire, and obtained most valuable information. He set a splendid example of courage and determination."

The information was valuable enough in that it confirmed the exact location of Fritz's line. It turned out that mine was the only patrol that got as far as the German wire. All the others either lost their way or were fired on as they approached.

The following day the whole Division received orders to move forward and dig in two hundred yards from the Hun front line. In our battalion, A and B Companies went forward as the first line with C and D Companies in support. Ossy put me in charge of B Company, partly because I knew the way, and partly because it was a regulation that the Commander or second in command of each Company should be kept back when the Regiment went into action.

Again it was a very dark night although fortunately there was no rain. I led the way alongside the railway line to the curve; then branched off across country. In my zeal to get within two hundred yards of the enemy, I overestimated the distance the Hun trench was down the slope. I walked steadily on, the two Companies following me in single file. Suddenly I halted. With a rude shock I realised I had walked right up to the German wire.

Here was a pretty predicament. At any moment we might be discovered. If they turned a machine-gun on us the whole force might be wiped out. I passed back a terse order to lie down. Then I sent my sergeant-major crawling back to superintend the withdrawal of the men by sections from the rear. They were to retire behind the ridge and lie down under cover.

For the second night Fritz was keeping a very bad watch. Both Companies were able to withdraw without a casualty. When the last section was safely back, my runner Reggie and I paced a distance of exactly two hundred yards from the German entanglements. Then we brought the men forward by sections and set them to work.

We laboured all night to entrench ourselves. Fritz did not tumble to the fact that there was anything unusual going on until we had been working for over an hour. Then he began spasmodic bursts of machine-gun fire. His guns were firing high, however, which, coupled with the fact that we were throwing up an earthwork in front of us, prevented more than a few casualties.

All night long I expected the battalion on our left to move forward and join on to the end of our new trench. They did not appear. I went along to see Alf Hawes, commanding A Company on the right. Nobody had connected with him either. At last came the dawn and to our astonishment we were the only troops in sight. On the whole slope there was not another British soldier to be seen. Our two Companies were opposing the whole of the Hindenburg Line by themselves.

I was rather worried by the situation. The Huns could not do very much during the day except shell us because they were unable to pass their own compact wire entanglements. But when night fell, I could visualise a strong force emerging through their pathway in the wire and surrounding us. I must make some provision against surprise.

We were about two hundred yards from the crest of the slope. I decided to make a dash for it and go back to discuss the position with Ossy. I ran as fast as I could, zig-zagging from side to side. They fired a few bullets at me but I got over the crest in safety. Ossy was naturally very concerned at our isolation and decided to send me to Brigade Headquarters to explain the situation to the Brigadier.

At Brigade they told me I should have to wait as the Brigadier was engaged with the Commanding Officer of the battalion who should have come up on my left. I decided to take the bull by the horns and burst into the presence. The Colonel was just reporting that his unit had dug in according to orders.

" Excuse me, sir," I interrupted him. " Your front line Companies may be dug in but they are not in sight of the enemy."

" Are yours ? " asked the General succinctly.

" Yes, sir. Both our Companies are dug in according to orders ; two hundred yards from the enemy front line."

" How do you know they are two hundred yards from the enemy ? " asked the Colonel, sarcastically. He did not dream that I had come out of the front line trench in broad daylight.

" Because I paced the distance myself," I replied crushingly.

The General roared with laughter and made me tell him the whole story. The Colonel was the first to agree that his men were at fault. He was a magnificent fellow, for whom I always had the greatest respect. It was not his fault that he had received an erroneous report from the officers under him. It turned out that they had encountered the entanglements of an abandoned trench and had mistaken it in the dark for their objective.

The General promised that we should be properly supported that night and I returned to the trench. As soon after dusk as possible I placed a Lewis gun in a shell-hole about two hundred yards on my flank and arranged for Alf Hawes to do the same on the right. It would probably be some hours before the troops moved forward to fill up the gap and I wanted to be prepared.

My anticipation that the Huns would make an attempt to surround us proved to be correct. Some half an hour later the gun on my flank opened fire. I at once went out to see what target they had found. A strong party of Huns had emerged from the wire almost in front of them. They were able to disperse that assault before it materialised. Shortly afterwards long lines of troops joined up with us and we were safe.

We stayed in the front line another two days and then went back to the Black line in support. The artillery was already active preparing for the assault on the Hindenburg Line. The wire required a great deal of attention to make sure it was cut properly, and it was not until the 23rd that the attack was launched.

Although we were detailed to support the first wave the date augured well for our Regiment to distinguish itself. St. George's Day and St. George is our patron saint. We spent the night before lined up behind an embankment. We were told that we should probably not be required, but I for one sincerely hoped otherwise. In a way I looked on this part of the Hindenburg Line as my property. It was too bad that we were not to make the actual assault.

It was touch and go that I was there at all. By rights it was George Thorpe's turn as he was out of the previous turn up the line. However, Ossy ordained that I was to command the Company so all was well.

The barrage was terrific and it seemed impossible that anything could stand up against it. Nevertheless, the wire was very tenacious and a good bit of it was still standing when the assault first went over. The position was held by the fifth battalion of the Prussian Guard, who were a pretty stubborn crowd. They put up an obstinate resistance.

It was not very long before we were required. A Company went first, but a few minutes later a call came for us and I moved forward. As we approached the position I could see the long lines of uncut wire with dead fusiliers hanging across it like pearls in a necklace where the Hun machine-guns had caught them. All the same some of them had penetrated through the gaps and the trench was captured. I had my usual luck and got my Company through the enemy's counter-barrage without any casualties. My men were full of fight and I led them right through A Company and cleared the

212

position up to the railway which was the boundary of our objective. There was no resistance ; the few Huns we encountered surrendered instantly. At once I set about preparing the trench for the counter-attack which I knew would follow. The whole place was a shambles, Huns and British mixed up together. Fritz had made good use of his island traverses and there were several places where he had slipped round the back and caught the attackers unawares.

The town of Gavrelle was a few hundred yards on our right. The attacking troops had gone right through and our right consequently projected slightly beyond our left. We were the extreme left of the Divisional front. The Division on our left whose main attack was directed against Oppy Wood had failed with the result that the position was held in echelon.

Twelve kilometres ahead of us I could see the spire of Douai Church. Between us and it there was not a single German trench. We had captured their last line of defence. If only the attack had been successful on a wider front. We could have pushed forward. If—what a big word it is !

CHAPTER ELEVEN

TWO V.C.'s

THE counter-attack was not launched until the following morning. The Huns were waiting to bring up their reserves. When they did start they kept on attacking all day long. Time after time long lines of men in field grey appeared over the crest of the ridge only to be swept away before they had descended half way down the slope. In siting the trench they had chosen an excellent position for defence against us, but, as the reverse slope was longer, it served us even better for defence against them. Never once did they get within a hundred yards of us.

I was once more in charge of the Company. Poor old George, who had come up to take over from me after we had consolidated the position, was sniped just before dusk. Fritz had dropped two machine-guns in his flight about two hundred yards in front of the trench. For some reason which I shall never be able to explain, George set out, without a word to anybody, to try and recover them. He managed to crawl up to them but that was all. A Hun got him with a bullet. We fetched him in just after dark, but I could see at once that there was no hope.

We went back to the Black line on the evening of the 24th. What was to happen next ? That was the question that filled our minds. We were so near to breaking through we were all keyed up for the next move. It was impossible that the authorities would let things rest where they were.

I discussed the matter with Ossy. He explained that the attack had not been successful on a sufficiently wide front. Oppy Wood was strongly fortified and had so far proved too much for the Division on our left. On our right, too, the chemical works at Monchy were a hard nut to crack. It would be folly to advance until the gap in the enemy's defences was sufficiently wide.

The following day he showed me some aerial photographs. Already the Huns were throwing up fresh trenches behind the ridge. Already they had placed fresh obstacles between us and Douai. I groaned with disappointment. If only we could have gone on. To be so near and yet so far.

On the 27th we received orders to go back again to the front line. The Division on our left were to make another attempt on Oppy. There was a preliminary wire-cutting barrage the following morning. Bill Haine, commanding C Company, took advantage of it and nipped over about thirty yards of open and took a strong point of the Huns that was bothering him. He brought in fifty prisoners and two machine-guns. From them we learned that the troops opposing us were the fifth battalion of the Prussian Guard. They were largely recruited from Berlin University, and were rather a fine crowd of men. Most of them could speak perfect English.

Bill found one of them lying wounded in a dug-out in the strong point. He said he was hungry, so tender-hearted William gave him a meal. Shortly afterwards, Bill and his party were forced to retire through a strong counter-attack. Bill retook the strong point the following morning. The wounded man was still there. He remarked naïvely that his compatriots were so busy keeping Bill from recapturing the position that they had not found time to give him anything to eat since their arrival. This appealed to Bill's sense of humour. He gave the fellow another meal and sent him to hospital on a stretcher.

Bill's private war lasted for nearly two days. The strong point in the hands of the enemy was a constant menace to our position. It gave them a convenient jumping off point from which they might have suddenly issued and cut off the whole of C Company and probably D as well. Sturdy William, who had been out with the Regiment since 1914 and who was still only twenty years of age, was not the man to leave his Company in danger. He kept on attacking that strong point until he had made sure that the advantage lay with us and not with the enemy. They gave him a Victoria Cross which he thoroughly well deserved. I quote the *Official Gazette* :

" Second Lieutenant Reginald Leonard Haine, H.A.C. For most conspicuous bravery and determination, when our troops, occupying a pronounced salient, were repeatedly counter-attacked. There was an ever present danger that if the enemy attack succeeded, the garrison of the salient would be surrounded.

Second Lieutenant Haine organised and led with the utmost gallantry six bombing attacks against a strong point which dangerously threatened our communication, capturing the position together with fifty prisoners and two machine-guns.

The enemy then counter-attacked with a battalion of the Guard, succeeded in regaining his position, and the situation appeared critical.

Second Lieutenant Haine at once formed a block in his trench, and for the whole of the following night maintained his position against repeated determined attacks.

Reorganising his men on the following morning, he again attacked and captured the strong point, pressing the enemy back for several hundred yards, and thus relieving the situation.

Throughout these operations, this officer's superb courage, quick decision and sound judgment were beyond praise, and it was his splendid personal example which inspired his men to continue their efforts during more than thirty hours of continuous fighting."

I was asleep during the night that Bill was keeping the enemy at bay. Orders were issued that our Division would attack at the same time as the Division on the left. By making a big show of it the authorities hoped to carry the whole line considerably further forward. The troops engaged in the assault for the Naval Division were the first and second battalions of the Royal Marines, than whom there are no finer troops in the British Army. I was in support to the First Battalion Royal Marines and did not anticipate that I should have anything to do at all. Consequently I disposed the whole of my Company in dug-outs and, retiring to my own, relaxed into much needed slumber.

I slept right through the barrage and the initial onslaught. I should probably have gone on sleeping for hours had not a runner from Headquarters arrived to awake me. He bore a curt message to immediately form a defensive flank. In an instant I was outside my dug-out. There was no time to enquire what had happened. It was obvious that something had gone wrong. I must act at once.

I gave hurried orders to Ernest Samuel, my second in command, to arrange the troops in a series of shell-holes diagonal to our former position. Waiting only to see the first sections clamber out of the trench to find their positions I moved along the trench towards Oppy with the idea of attempting to discover what had taken place which jeopardised our flank.

The first thing that struck me was the curious hush in the atmosphere. Neither guns nor rifles were firing. It was just like the temporary cessation in a thunderstorm when the forces of nature seem to pause before bursting out afresh with greater fury than before. The sun was shining and everything appeared ridiculously peaceful. All the same my heart was beating wildly

under an impulse for which I could not account. My
instinct told me we were in deadly danger.

Ahead I could make out the Marines in their objective.
They had not failed then. But what about the troops
on our left ? They had undoubtedly reached the trench
which had baffled them before. I could see them in
position. What then had thrown us on the defensive ?
It could only be that they had failed to advance further
to draw level with the Marines.

I was at the limit of my own trench, which was the
extreme left of the Divisional front, wondering what I
should do next. Suddenly a bombing attack started
from the direction of Oppy Wood. Bang ! Bang !
Zunk ! Zunk ! I could see the smoke from the
explosions nearly a mile away. Fritz was attacking
down the trench.

It went on for some five minutes without making any
appreciable headway. Then, without any warning, and
without any direct attack being made on them, all the
troops between me and the curls of grey smoke in the
distance left their trench and ran back towards the
position they had started from at dawn.

Panic ! Sheer unaccountable panic ! As inexplicable
as it was unpremeditated. The sort of thing the greatest
psychologist in the world could not explain ; a sudden
terror which affected the whole force simultaneously.
It was a sight I hope I never see again. For a brief
moment it had its effect on me. I felt my knees knocking
together under me. I was obliged to clutch at the
parapet to prevent myself from falling. Then the
thought fired my brain that with all the troops having
cleared out between me and the enemy in a few minutes
my own Company would be assailed. And if we failed
to stem the victorious torrent of the Huns the whole
of the left of our Division would crumple up like a leaf.

How long I remained there shaking I cannot say. It
seemed like some minutes ; actually it could not have

been more than a few seconds. Then the curious feeling came to me which I have described before that I was no longer acting under my own volition. Something outside myself, greater than I, seemed to take charge of me. Acting under this mysterious influence I ran forward.

Already officers of the terrorised troops were attempting to rally them. I found a handful who were still in possession of their senses. I arranged as many as I encountered in shell-holes to right and left of the trench and ordered them to fire their rifles. I did not care a damn whether or not they hit anything. There is nothing so soothing to the nerves as to be doing something. My antidote to their panic was to make them shoot. Encouraged by the example of the few I had rallied others joined them. Soon I had a moderate force spread out in an arc. They were steady now and I had no further fear of a fresh withdrawal. The British Tommy does not do that sort of thing twice in a morning.

With the defence organised and the knowledge that my own stalwart Company was in support to back them up, I turned my attention to finding out how far the Hun attack had been successful. The bombing had now ceased, from which I inferred that Fritz had overcome the resistance in his path.

Two of my own men had followed me down the trench. My runner, Reggie Hughesdon, as in duty bound, and Lance-Corporal Scharlach. Why he had accompanied me I do not know to this day. At the time I did not stop to enquire. I was only too thankful to have two men on whom I could rely implicitly. Both were trained bombers.

My instructions to them before I started were very simple. Each had a Mills bomb in his hand with the safety pin out. I told them that if I fired my pistol they were to throw their bombs immediately to pitch about fifteen yards in front of me. This would land them in the next traverse in front of where we were. They only had two bombs each and, at the time, I gave no thought as to where we might find a further supply.

These preparations only took a few seconds and we were on the move almost at once. The trench was quite empty and we were able to move forward fairly rapidly. Round traverse after traverse we dodged, I with my revolver held ready for instant action. In the first hundred yards we encountered nobody. We were now well in advance of all British troops, and the noise of my improvised defence was receding in the distance. I could hear them still firing, but only one of them had followed me. He was a private in one of the battalions of the Royal Fusiliers, and he made the fourth member of my little army.

We covered another hundred yards without resistance. Then suddenly, as I entered one end of a stretch of trench between two traverses, a big Hun entered the other, rifle and bayonet in his hand. I fired ; he dropped his rifle and clapped both his hands to his stomach. Almost instantaneously with my shot I heard the whizz of Reggie's bomb as it passed over my head. A second man appeared behind the first ; I fired again and he dropped like a stone. Bang ! Bang ! The two bombs thrown by my followers exploded one after the other.

The third man saw the fate of his two predecessors and turned to go back. Those behind, not knowing what had happened tried to come forward. I fired again. Bang ! Zunk ! went the remaining bombs of our small store. That was enough. The next instant the Hun attack was in full retreat.

We followed as fast as we could. Discretion had gone to the winds or I should have realised the utter foolishness of running as fast as I could into the enemy's territory with only three men to support me. But my blood was up. I felt a thrill only comparable to running through the opposition at Rugger to score a try.

In and out we went round traverse after traverse.

Every now and again I caught a glimpse of field grey disappearing round the corner ahead. Twice I fired, but I was running too hard to take careful aim. At last I came to a place where a shell had blown the parapet right across the trench, forming a natural barricade. My brain told me we had come far enough. I stopped.

Knowing the Huns' little ways I expected to be counter-attacked as soon as he had rallied his troops. I at once started putting my strong point in a condition of defence. The fusilier knew nothing of bombs so I stationed him on the look-out beside the barricade. We furnished him with seven rifles, some Hun and some British, all fully loaded. Even then, I could not help thinking of Robinson Crusoe's similar preparations.

The rest of us collected all the bombs we could find. Fortunately the trench was well provided, though, of course, all the bombs were German. Strange though it may seem I was glad of this. One can throw a German bomb farther than a British.

The reason for this is quite a simple one. The Hun bomb is a canister full of high explosive on the end of a short stick. It relies for its accomplishment mostly on moral effect. It weighs one pound. The Mills bomb on the other hand is designed to do considerable damage when it bursts. It consists of a serrated cast-iron body filled with two and a half ounces of ammonal. It weighs a pound and a half. One can throw a pound weight with a stick to act as a lever very much farther than one can throw a pound and a half of dead weight. Certainly the Mills bomb is a much superior weapon when it happens to explode in a trench, but in the excitement of a bombing attack the vast majority fall on the top or outside the parapet. The greater noise of the Hun canister when exploding has a far greater effect in the long run than the few more dangerous Mills bombs which fall on their objective.

It was less than ten minutes before the Huns returned.

When they came they were determined to retrieve the ground they had lost. I could tell that by the vigour of their attack. Right from the first bombs fell thick and fast. We three replied with as good as we received.

I threw off my tin hat to give my arms better play for throwing. Next went my gas mask. Bang! Bang! Bang! Bang! The air was thick with bombs going and coming. Those that fell in the trench we flung over the parapet before they had time to explode. My two companions were magnificent. Our fusilier friend protected our front.

Reggie suddenly drew my attention to our fast failing supply of missiles. " Hadn't we better retire ? " he suggested.

" I'm not going back one foot, Reggie," I cried. " If we run out of bombs, we'll keep them out with rifles."

Fortunately we did not have to resort to such a desperate measure. The Hun attack ceased as suddenly as it had started. We were still undefeated, but we only had six bombs left.

If Fritz had only known. For that matter if he had known we were only four he would have undoubtedly rushed us over the top. That was the tremendous luck of the whole affair. He did not know. He failed to take a chance. His failure cost him the position.

Not that I thought he had given up trying. Our respite was only a breathing space. We employed it in going back along the trench and collecting more ammunition. We were once more ready for him when a welcome face appeared round the traverse behind us.

" Hallo, Alf ! " cried Sammy. " I thought I had better bring the Company along to lend you a hand."

" Have you brought any bombs ? " I asked quickly. Sammy laughed.

" As many as we could carry," he chuckled. " I knew you would want them."

Good old Sammy ! His cool brain never failed in an

emergency. He is one of the finest fellows I have ever known. He hated war, mud, discomfort, but he served throughout the whole campaign with the greatest cheerfulness, always ready to carry out his orders to the letter. If his ancestors amongst the fighting tribes of Israel were able to watch their child conduct himself during the greatest conflict the world has ever known they must have rattled their ghostly spears in pride of their worthy descendant.

I quickly made my dispositions. I placed Lewis guns in shell-holes fifty yards on either side of the trench with instructions to fire ahead of us across the trench. Scharlach was provided with rifle grenades which would fire about sixty yards ahead. I arranged another corporal with another type of rifle-grenade to drop about one hundred and twenty yards ahead. Reggie and I would throw hand grenades.

We had not very long to wait for the second attack but it only lasted about five minutes. The rifle grenades bothered the Hun line of communications and the Lewis guns prevented them from getting out over the top. They soon had enough of us.

I left Sammy in charge of the strong point and went back to rally the battalions who should have been occupying the position. When I was assured that their temper was now sufficiently strong for them to be left I handed over the position to them and withdrew my Company to their former trench.

The Brigadier sent me a telegram during the day, placing me in command of the trench and bidding all officers concerned carry out my orders. I sent out patrols to occupy shell-holes some two hundred yards in front of the position and generally made the position quite secure. But Fritz left us severely alone.

The three men with me were given Distinguished Conduct Medals. Unfortunately the fusilier was killed by a shell on the following day so his was awarded posthumously. In due course I received the Victoria Cross. The following is the announcement in the *Gazette :*

" Second Lieutenant Alfred Oliver Pollard, M.C., H.A.C. For most conspicuous bravery and determination.

The troops of various units on the left of this officer's battalion had become disorganized owing to the heavy casualties from shell-fire ; and a subsequent determined enemy attack with very strong forces caused further confusion and retirement, closely pressed by hostile forces.

Second Lieutenant Pollard at once realised the seriousness of the situation, and dashed up to stop the retirement. With only four men he started a counter-attack with bombs, and pressed it home till he had broken the enemy attack, regained all that had been lost and much ground in addition.

The enemy retired in disorder, sustaining many casualties.

By his force of will, dash, and splendid example, coupled with an utter contempt of danger, this officer, who has already won the D.C.M. and M.C., infused courage into every man who saw him."

We were relieved that night. It was a Divisional relief and we went right back to a camp under canvas just outside Arras. Reggie and I nearly lost our lives on the way down. Fritz was sending over gas-shells and I could not be bothered to put on my gas-mask. I was too tired. When we reached the spot where the cookers had come out to meet the battalion with hot tea, we were both violently sick. The hot tea had the effect of clearing the gas out of us—fortunately.

Ossy had something to say to both Bill and me that night. We had added a chapter to the history of one of the most famous Regiments in the world. I was very proud to have had a hand in it, but I have often wondered what would have happened had Fritz come over the top instead of sticking to the trench.

CHAPTER ONE

I BECOME ENGAGED

WHEN the Divisional General inspected us on the morning of the 30th April, 1917, we had reached the climax of our fame. Never in the hundreds of years of history in which the Regiment had been involved had our lustre shone more brightly. We had been severely tested throughout the past fortnight and we had emerged covered in honour and glory. From the Commanding Officer down to the latest joined recruit, all had pulled their weight; every man had stood up to the demands made of him. We were a perfectly united team. All were comrades who understood and appreciated the part each had played.

Bill Haine and I naturally came in for a slightly greater meed of praise than the others. We were recommended for the Victoria Cross. According to the General we had been instrumental in saving the left of the Division. Had we failed in our respective tasks there is little doubt that our flank would have crumpled and the Division would have been badly cut up. But both Bill and I fully appreciated that we should have accomplished nothing without the backing of our men.

We were a joyous company when we were dismissed from the formality of parade. In the Mess everyone congratulated everyone else. Laughter was prevalent. The General stayed to lunch, and, unbending for once from the dignity of his position, made himself extremely agreeable.

Now, it so happens that my birthday is on the fourth of May. Knowing of this the battalion wag dared me to ask the General whether we might borrow the Marines band to play during the afternoon. My request was granted without demur and in due course the band arrived.

The Royal Marines band from the Chatham depot is always worth hearing. The day was glorious, and all the boys were able to lounge about on the grass and get the full benefit of the treat. Under the command of Musical Director Hobey it gave us three hours of delightful music.

Arrangements were made by the Mess for our visitors to have as much liquid refreshment as they wanted. That was all right with regard to the band itself, but it was taken too literally by the driver of the lorry who brought them from Divisional Headquarters, some seven miles away. The band was due to be back to play at the General's Mess at seven o'clock in the evening. It never arrived. The alcohol which the driver had imbibed bubbled up inside him and caused him to deposit the whole outfit in a ditch miles from anywhere.

That was bad enough in itself, but there was worse to follow. I wrote a short note of thanks. Not liking to send it to the General himself, I addressed it to Colonel Aspinall, the G.S.O.1.

DEAR COLONEL ASPINALL,

I shall be glad if you will convey to the General my grateful thanks for lending the band on my birthday. The whole battalion enjoyed it immensely.

I merely dropped the envelope in the battalion letter box in the ordinary way. It got as far as Brigade, where some bright spark, seeing it addressed to the G.S.O.1. of the Division, fished it out of the usual post-bag and despatched it by special runner. It reached Divisional Headquarters at two o'clock in the morning, and they woke the Colonel up to give it to him. I should have loved to have heard what he said.

The Division moved further back for rest and reorganisation shortly afterwards. I went on leave. There was nothing special about it. It happened to be my turn on the roster. The particular episode that marked this leave as being different from all others was that I broke my promise to My Lady.

How it came about I cannot say. Thinking it over since I have decided that the impulse that moved me must have been a sudden overflow of pent-up emotion. For more than a year I had been harbouring a passion that possessed my whole being. Possibly because I had had very little opportunity of mixing with the opposite sex in the meantime the pedestal I had erected in my heart had reached abnormal proportions. The excitement of leave, the expectation of receiving the highest honour I could attain, the reputation I had earned as a fighter, the knowledge that I stood high in the regard of my comrades in the battalion all had their part in carrying me away.

She and her two sisters were staying in my mother's house. I was due to return to France in a couple of days. It was late at night. Most of the party had gone to bed. Somehow She and I were left alone together. Something welled up within me. I took her in my arms. In a rush of half coherent phrases I told her how much I loved her ; how badly I wanted her ; that I couldn't live without her.

She was bewildered by the suddenness of my attack. Even so she did not repulse me. Neither did she embrace me. She suggested quite sensibly that we had better sleep the night on it and talk it over quietly in the morning.

Morning came at last. After breakfast we went for

a country walk. There was ample opportunity for discussion. I expounded the simple fact that I had never loved anyone in my life but Her. She, for her part, declared quite frankly that she did not love me, or anyone else for that matter ; that she really had not had any intention whatever of getting married, but that she would think it over very carefully and let me know her decision. She told me she liked me as much as any man she knew ; that she trusted me ; and that as I loved her as much as I did, it hardly seemed fair to disappoint me. No doubt if we did marry, she would learn to love me afterwards. We kissed once. The following day I went back to France.

The Division were still at rest and there was no talk of returning to the line at present. We spent our time in fatigues of various kinds. We were lying at Roclincourt, just outside Arras, and our sole diversion off duty was a visit to the Officers' Club, which had been newly opened. It really belonged to the Sixth Corps, and as we were of the Thirteenth we were not supposed to use it, but no one ever protested to my knowledge.

I had two things on my mind. Would I receive a V.C. ; what would be Her decision ? I speculated for hours on both.

News of the V.C. arrived first. On the sixth of June the battalion went mad. Bill and I were gazetted. The first two V.C.'s the Regiment had ever been awarded. There must be a suitable celebration.

The Mess Secretary went into Arras and bought up every drink he could lay hands on. The result was a glorious binge. Everyone got tight from the Commanding Officer downwards. It was a most thorough business.

A few days later I received my other answer. She would marry me. We were engaged. I had the V.C., and now I was engaged to the most glorious girl in the

world. Did ever man's cup of happiness brim fuller ?
I did not think so—then.

But although I myself was as happy as the day was
long a cloud had settled on the battalion. Ossy was
superseded by an officer sent out from home—Lieutenant
Colonel P. C. Cooper. It was a most unfortunate
happening.

Looking at the whole affair with an impartial mind
from the distance of time, I do not see how any blame
can be attached to P. C. He was merely a very senior
officer, who, although he crossed the water with us in
1914, was invalided home before we got into action
and was kept at home right up to May 1917. That
he was senior to our beloved Ossy was a matter of
chance and the fault of the system which insists on
promotion in time of war by seniority instead of by
merit. Not that I am questioning P. C.'s merit. He
was very capable in some directions. No one can judge
of his ability in the line. He was never in it when an
action was in progress and only for a short time in
ordinary trench routine.

His fault was that he arrived to supersede Ossy. Had
he been any other man, with the single exception of
Colonel Treffry, the result would have been the same.
We wanted Ossy and we were not prepared to transfer
our loyalty. Nevertheless in spite of all our fuming,
Ossy went down to Major ; Bun Morphy returned to
the command of C Company ; and P. C. took control.

Bill and I went on leave shortly afterwards. That I
went was a miracle, or shall I more truthfully write, a
wangle. I had only been back from my other leave
three weeks. But the authorities decided that as Bill
would probably receive his decoration I ought to be
with him. I was in the seventh heaven. I was going
to see my fiancée so much sooner than I had anticipated.
We had so much to say to one another ; so many plans
to make ; a ring to buy. Life was marvellous.

231

CHAPTER TWO

BUCKINGHAM PALACE

WHAT a time we had that leave! Two care-free boys in London. Everyone wanted to entertain us. We had lunch and dinner invitations three deep some times. It was much better fun being two than one. One by himself might have felt shy or overwhelmed. With two it was possible to exchange notes and share jests unknown to the others. There was also a psychological effect in having some support.

If our heads were to be turned they would have been turned then. Did we attempt to buy a drink in the interval at the theatre someone would thrust himself forward and insist on paying for it. If we showed up at the Piccadilly Hotel—our favourite haunt—for a meal, the head waiter would unctuously escort us past the inevitable queue to a table in the centre of the room. Everyone paid us homage. There would undoubtedly have been an excuse had we assumed we were some sort of superior beings. Fortunately we were both sufficiently level-headed to appraise the plaudits of the mob at their true worth.

We had one experience which amused us both very much. We were sitting in a train at Victoria waiting for it to start. The time for its departure arrived and passed. Nothing happened. Bill got out to see what was causing the delay. Except for one or two officials the platform was deserted. Everyone was clustered at the far end of the train gazing into the sky. The Huns were raiding London.

This was too good to miss. To us an air raid was like a busman's holiday. We hurried eagerly to a point of vantage.

There they were. A small flight of aeroplanes amongst the clouds. They were the deuce of a way up, far too high for any effective target practice. The anti-aircraft guns which formed part of the defence of London were firing for all they were worth without the faintest chance of hitting anything.

Someone remarked on the terrible barrage. That was what amused us. Compared with an artillery barrage in preparation for an attack it was like a boy's air-gun being likened to a fifteen-inch howitzer.

Of course I spent a lot of my time with My Lady. She was staying with us too, so that we did not have to miss a single day without seeing one another. How proud I was to escort her when we went to town. One of our expeditions was for the purchase of the ring. She chose a black pearl set in diamonds on a platinum ring.

Normally we should have returned to France at the end of a fortnight. But a big investiture was arranged for the twenty-first of July and we were bidden to remain for it. That gave us a month in all.

We decided it would be rather jolly to spend a few days by the sea. After the usual discussion about where to go we selected Sandown. The party consisted of my fiancée, my youngest sister, Bill and myself. We put up at the Sandown Hotel.

The War seemed very far away from there. Bathing and boating in the day time ; country walks and concerts at night ; our holiday was a most delightful interlude.

All the same an incident occurred which should have warned both My Lady and I how totally unsuited we were in temperament. One evening after dinner we had walked rather further than usual. My Lady was a trifle tired, and to save her as much as possible I suggested attempting a short cut across some fields to where we could see the hotel in the distance. She hesitated for a moment, asking me if I were sure we could get through. Without in the least knowing the country I was positive we could. We nearly did but within a quarter of a mile of our objective we encountered a thirty-foot drainage dyke.

Here was the devil to pay. To go back meant a detour of nearly three miles. To go forward without wading was impossible. She was furious. Over-tired, she accused me of not taking proper care of her. I ought not to have taken that way unless I was sure we could pass. I was thoughtless, inconsiderate and neglectful. For my part I could not see what there was to make a fuss about. To me a short cut across country was an adventure. Even had she not been tired I should probably have suggested trying it as a matter of course. It was unfortunate that we had met such an obstacle but it was not insurmountable. I would willingly wade through with her in my arms.

I was bewildered by her point of view; she utterly failed to understand mine. Both of us were right according to our temperaments. It was against her nature to take a step in the dark. I almost invariably acted on impulse. In the end we went back the way we had come and round by the road. We walked in silence. The following day I apologised and was forgiven and we resumed our companionship.

Had I been gifted with the power to see into the future I should have broken off the engagement then and there. No happiness can result when two strong natures are hopelessly incompatible. But I was madly, desperately in love. That was why I gave in and apologised instead of insisting that in following my instinct I was equally in the right with her. She had the advantage in that she was not in love with me, therefore she did not experience that supreme desire to save the one she loved

234

from even a momentary unhappiness. I gave in then and I gave in many times afterwards but it was from strength rather than weakness. I hated her to be distressed.

It would all come right when we were married. That was the slogan with which I consoled myself. In the meantime I was on leave. When I went back to France I might never return. Live for to-day; let to-morrow take care of itself.

We all enjoyed that holiday. The weather was perfect. We were all sorry when we had to return to town. But our leave was drawing to an end. We were to attend at Buckingham Palace on the Saturday; the following day we returned to the battalion.

The investiture was a very impressive affair. It was for V.C.'s only—twenty-four in all. Eighteen attended; the others were posthumous awards. We formed up in the courtyard in the front of the Palace. Each of us had had a hook or hooks fastened into his tunic by an official on his arrival. The Grenadiers mounted a guard of honour. Until His Majesty arrived surrounded by a group of A.D.C.'s, the band played as only a Guard's band can.

At last a sharp word of command brought the Guard of Honour to rigid attention. We followed suit. "Present arms!" The ensigns dipped. The band played the most stirring tune in the world—the British National Anthem. His Majesty emerged from the Palace.

I stood with my arms straight down by my sides and my chest swelling my tunic. "God save our gracious King." Wasn't that what we were fighting for? To save the King and all he stood for—our great Nation? From the highest in the land whose representatives surrounded their monarch to the middle class and the lowest who formed the crowd pressed against the railings of the forecourt, all were epitomized in that gathering. We represented the Navy, the Army and the Air Force. We even represented those who were fallen in the little group of relatives of those to be posthumously honoured at the end of our line.

" Send Him victorious, happy and glorious." Well, he would be victorious if human endeavour could make him so. Every one of us had done his damnedest and we were there to receive our rewards. Not that we needed them. People do not go into action with the idea of winning the Victoria Cross. They go with the bare intention of doing their duty. The decoration merely happens.

" Stand at ease ! " The tension relaxed, the proceedings commenced. We were called out in order of seniority. I was the sixth. Ten paces forward and I halted in front of my King. Colonel Clive Wigram read out the particulars of my deeds as published in the Gazette. I stood stiffly at attention. When the recitation was concluded His Majesty hooked my medals on to their hooks.

" I've followed the doings of your battalion with the greatest interest," he said. " I'm very proud indeed to be your Captain-General and Colonel."

He shook my hand with a grip of iron. I had scratched the back of my hand rather badly against a rock at the seaside. The scar had only just formed. His Majesty's hand clasp was so powerful that the wound had burst open afresh. I still have the scar. Every time I look at it I am reminded of the occasion when I was so highly honoured.

I stepped back, saluted, and returned to my place to watch Bill going through the same ordeal.

At last it was over and we were in a taxi speeding down the Mall. We were to be given a lunch at Armoury House, Regimental Headquarters. That was all right. What we had not anticipated was the reception we received. As we entered the gates we found the band

drawn up waiting for us. We were made to march
behind them between two lines of yelling troops to
where a platform had been improvised on a couple
of carts in the middle of the grounds. I never felt such
a fool in my life.

Colonel Lord Denbigh and Colonel Treffry made us
get up on the platform whilst they both made speeches.
Then we were supposed to speak but we got out of that.
At last we succeeded in escaping to the bar.

Even here we were not safe. Someone came along
and complained that we were keeping the luncheon
party waiting. We were dragged downstairs. The
lunch was all right but there were more speeches to
follow. Colonel Lord Denbigh made a long one recount-
ing the activities of the battalions and batteries who
were at the front. Then there was a pause and someone
whispered in my ear that I was expected to reply.
Well, up to then I had scarcely made a speech in my
life so I stood up and said :

" Thank you very much everybody."

Then I sat down again. They did not seem to think
a lot of my effort so they had a cut at Bill. Bill stood
up and said :

" I think Alf's said all there is to say."

Then he sat down. I suppose we had knocked the
proceedings rather flat for we had peace and quiet for
awhile. Not for very long though. Colonel Treffry had
to have his turn. Then our fathers enjoyed a little
reflected glory by saying a few words each. I suppose
one must allow them a certain amount of rope on an
occasion like that. Fortunately they kept within
bounds. Neither Bill nor I would have stood listening
to a moving word picture of the hero, aged six.

General Sir Henry McKinnon made a speech too. I
only remember one thing he said. He mentioned that
he was a Grenadier. " If ever either of you boys are
anywhere near a Grenadiers Mess in France, pop in

for a drink. Just say General McKinnon sent you." The sentiment was a noble one but I could not help wondering what sort of reception we should have received had we taken the suggestion seriously.

The affair was over at last and we were free. We promptly dashed off to the West End to meet my sister and My Lady. One final dinner party at the Piccadilly ; a box at " Cheep " ; a night of gaiety. The following day we returned to France.

CHAPTER THREE

THE FIRST AMERICANS

WE rejoined the battalion to find it in very changed circumstances. During our month's leave it had left the Naval Division and been drafted to General Headquarters. Two Companies were stationed at Montreuil, one at advanced G.H.Q., whilst battalion headquarters and the remaining Company were at Hesdin. I should have liked to have stayed at Montreuil where Ossy was in command of the detachment, but as B Company was at Hesdin I had to join them. Bill went up to advanced G.H.Q., so I did not see him again for some time.

The troops were billeted in a French barracks whilst we occupied the Mess. For some things I was quite glad to be out of the line for a while, if only to get used to my new-found happiness. I had heard it said before that fellows who had a girl at home thinking of them were less keen on taking risks than the totally unattached. I had always pooh-poohed the suggestion as being fantastic. Now, to my utter astonishment, I found there was something in it. It occurred to me that if I were killed, My Lady might be grieved. And because I wished her nothing but happiness, I was glad that for a while she would have no cause to worry.

I did not want us to be out of action for good though. When the end of the War arrived—if ever it did arrive— I wanted to be in the thick of it. A rest in the country in the summer-time was very, very nice—for a time. But it must not be too long. Nothing is so boring as inactivity. I decided to consult "Uncle George," our Regimental oracle on all matters pertaining to the Service.

Major G. H. Mayhew, M.C., our Quartermaster, has spent the whole of his life in the Army. To us he was not the ordinary quartermaster responsible only for his particular job. He was our father and mother, guide, philosopher and friend. Privileged people addressed him as Uncle George. He was the terror of all who merited his displeasure and the pillar of all who needed his assistance. In his own province he was supreme. However short the notice of an intended move, Uncle George was never caught napping. Because of his popularity wherever he went, he could conjure up motor lorries like a magician producing rabbits from a hat. He always got there complete with stores.

He was vastly amused at my wanting to know when we should be returning to the line.

"Haven't you had enough of it yet, Alfred?" he chuckled. "I should have thought you'd done your share."

That was as far as I could get. He did not know. Nobody knew. We were at G.H.Q. with no settled programme. Some battalion had to be there to supply the necessary guards and duties. For the time being we were the chosen ones. Later we might be changed.

I am not going to recount our daily life at G.H.Q. Day succeeded day with monotonous regularity. Christmas came and passed. I began to wonder whether we should ever see the front line again.

Ossy then suggested that I went on a course of some sort. A change might do me good. Accordingly I put in for the next course available. It turned out to be for the Lewis Gun School at Le Touquet.

I enjoyed that Lewis Gun Course immensely. They made us work pretty hard but everything was well organised and decidedly interesting. We were divided into squads of eight under a sergeant-instructor. The squad to which I was allotted consisted of a very decent set of fellows. Two of them were Americans.

There were nineteen Americans altogether in the school. They were all picked officers who had been sent on ahead of their army to learn as much as possible about British methods. They were a quiet, studious crowd, more like a party of bank inspectors than soldiers. The questions they asked about everything under the sun. How did we manage to cook in a front line trench ? Was it true that the German officers had to drive their men into action at the point of the revolver ? They certainly wanted to know.

Of course they had their legs pulled unmercifully. If they believed all the yarns they were told they must have gleaned a very confused idea of modern warfare. I suppose it did not matter very much. They would soon know all about it for themselves.

I was guilty of organising a rag against them on New Year's Eve. The course began on the twenty-seventh of December, so we had had just five days to get to know one another. According to custom we British had a merry party to see the old year out. The Americans on the other hand carried on with their studies all the evening and retired to bed as usual at ten o'clock. It seemed to me that they might at least have thrown aside the dignity of being the advanced guard of the American Army for one night.

The sleeping quarters at the camp consisted of long narrow huts with a door at each end. The beds were arranged against the wall on either side with a passage down the centre. Close on one o'clock in the morning, I and three other fellows entered quietly by one door.

Working in pairs we rapidly turned over all the beds with their occupants enveloped in their blankets and flea-bags. The pandemonium was terrific. Irate sons of the United States were hitting out at one another in their desire for retaliation. By the time the first light went on we were clear at the opposite end of the hut.

They never found out who was responsible for their discomfiture, although they thought they did. I happened to sit next to one of them at lunch the following day and he told me all about it. I simulated tremendous indignation.

" Don't you worry, Loo-tenant," he reassured me. " We know the guy who was responsible. You just wait until to-night."

I waited in mingled amusement and trepidation. Nothing happened to me, but some unfortunate fellow who had not had any part in the affair got a fairly rough passage.

I worked jolly hard on that course. I wanted to show the battalion that I could excel out of the line as well as in it. Of course I had a big advantage over some of them in that I had had a lot of experience in choosing machine-gun positions and in handling the guns in action. The net result was that I passed out third with a distinguished certificate.

There was a revolver competition on the last day. We had to shoot six rounds deliberate and six rounds rapid with either hand. Just before we started the sergeant-instructor took me on one side and explained that it was usual for the senior officer in each squad to organise a sweepstake. I was the senior officer in ours so I arranged for a pool of five francs per head. We were all fairly level shooting with our right hands. When it came to the left, however, my score was more than double anybody else's. The practice I had put in when I was wounded stood me in good stead. But as the organiser of the sweep I felt decidedly embarrassed. It looked too much like a put-up job. I then discovered that it was also usual for the winner of the sweep to hand his winnings to the sergeant-instructor. As I had already bought a round of drinks in celebration which cost me ninety francs, I decided that another time I would sooner be the loser.

I returned to the battalion refreshed and invigorated. My ambition now was to accomplish the same in Lewis gun training that I had previously accomplished in bombing. I wanted to make every man in the battalion a trained Lewis gunner. I started with the men in C Company. Day after day I took a class. It was something to do at any rate, even though we never went near the line again. And then, just when I was really getting going we were moved to Montreuil.

Of course that upset everything. It was impossible to keep a class going with the interruptions caused by the guards and duties. So once more I found myself with practically nothing to do.

On the twenty-first of March the whole British Army got a bad scare. Fritz broke through at Cambrai. The first we knew of the affair was an urgent order to pack up and be prepared to move at half an hour's notice. It was very interesting to see the effect of the order on the various fellows in the battalion. Those who had not been up the line before were pleased; the others were divided into two classes. Some were down in the dumps, most were indifferent; a few like myself were frankly delighted. I was definitely filled with joy. After the terribly boring months through which I had just passed the prospect of some fighting was decidedly bracing.

For two days we were on tenter-hooks. Rumour succeeded rumour. The whole British Army was in retreat; arrangements were being made to defend the

Channel ports; Fritz had invented a new weapon for which we had no counter. In the battalion we expected our orders hourly. They never came.

The Field Marshal had gone to his advanced Headquarters immediately the alarm was given. On the second day he returned to Montreuil. The attack was held. The Huns might advance a few more miles but they would never break through.

I heard the news with mixed feelings. I was glad the German push had failed; I was deeply disappointed that we should not be required after all. If only we could have got away from G.H.Q. the chances were that we should have been kept in the Division we joined. As it was we were still there and there was nothing for it but to resume the deadly monotony of the daily round.

One day orders were received that four special platoons were to be trained to demonstrate British drill and British methods to the American Army which was just beginning to arrive. Ossy was to take charge of the training, which would be carried out on the sea coast not far from Etaples. The platoons had already been detailed, each under the command of its own officer. There remained only the question of an adjutant to assist Ossy. I immediately suggested myself, and to my great delight was appointed.

I started on my new duties with great zest and enthusiasm. Once again I was doing something which I felt was definitely helping to win the War instead of merely playing at it. In my ignorance I believed the Americans would jump at the chance to learn something from our experience. Those platoons must be trained to become living drill books. They were. When they were finally passed as ready they were as near perfection as hard work and human ingenuity could make them. Not that I am attempting to take the credit for turning them out. That must be shared amongst all their instructors, with Ossy receiving the lion's share. I merely did my own job to the best of my ability.

We had very little leisure during those weeks of intensive instruction. Everyone in the camp was hard at it from first thing in the morning until last thing at night. Even after the last parade was dismissed we used to hold discussions on how we could increase efficiency. Nothing was too much trouble.

At last the job was completed. The four platoons departed for different camps in the American training area. Ossy and I were left with our small staff in an empty camp.

We were expecting instructions to return to Montreuil when the news came through that the battalion had been relieved and were being transferred to a camp just outside Boulogne. It made a change certainly, but, with our numbers depleted by the training platoons it seemed improbable that we should have a chance of going back to the line.

Our new camp was entirely under canvas, but as we had now reached the commencement of summer we were quite comfortable. At first there was a great deal of speculation as to how we were to be employed. We were already running a small school for training officers. Was this to be increased ? To some extent it was, but at the same time we received instructions to supply a further six demonstration platoons.

Once more Ossy and I got busy with our organisation. With our previous experience we made rapid headway. If anything the training was better than before. The men were magnificent. They entered into the spirit of the thing in a way that made our work a pleasure.

The question which vexed my mind was what would be left for me to do after they had gone. The battalion would be a mere skeleton with far too many officers for the number of troops. I decided that I must go with some of the training platoons to the American

Army and persuaded Ossy to arrange for me to be put in charge of two of them. Quite apart from the fact that it would be interesting, I was certain I could be of use.

But before the training programme was completed an event took place that affected the whole current of my life. I applied for special leave, went home and got married.

CHAPTER FOUR

WITH THE AMERICAN ARMY

I FULLY expected the Americans to welcome us with open arms. They spoke the same language ; were descended in the original from the same stock ; had a common aim with us in beating the enemy. We had nearly four years of experience on the Western front which we were prepared to pass on for their benefit. To my utmost astonishment they did not want to listen. Right from the first their general attitude was that they knew as much about conducting a war as we did.

Almost the first day I was with them I made a casual remark to one of their officers to the effect that they were lucky to be able to profit by our mistakes. His reply enlightened me as to what I might expect.

" Ah, wal, loo-tenant, we don't need to be told anything. This Division's been under arms on the Mexican frontier since 1916. Our troops are as seasoned as any you've got here."

The Mexican frontier ! Ye Gods ! They had probably heard a couple of revolvers fired during the whole period. I wondered how they would appreciate the comparison with a modern artillery barrage as put down by Master Fritz when preparing to attack.

They did need to be told a lot, a tremendous lot, but at the same time there were things they could learn from them too. For instance their drill on active service put ours completely in the shade. To illustrate my meaning with one simple manœuvre. They would change a party of men on parade standing at ease into a column of fours on the march with one command.

" Sections right, hike ! "

The sections, previously numbered off in fours, simply wheeled round as in cavalry drill and marched off, shouldering their rifles as they did so. Most of their units did not bother about such niceties as the step, or working together, but does it really matter in time of war ? To give them their due I saw some of their crack battalions act on such a simple command with the utmost precision.

To get the same result our commands are legion : A cautionary word to get the men properly at ease ; " Attention " ; " Slope Arms " ; " Move to the right in Fours, Form Fours " ; " Right " ; " By the left, Quick March." Magnificently impressive in peace time and I would not have the detail altered for review purposes. But I think we must hand it to our cousins across the water for evolving an active service drill of a greater practical value.

We were saved from the fatal mistake we might have made had we tried to teach them anything. There was a British Brigadier in charge of their training who warned us of all probable pitfalls. He advised us to take the line that we were demonstrating British methods as a matter of interest without the slightest suggestion that our audience might profit from what they saw.

I could not help thinking what a pity it was that there should be such a lack of co-operation between the two armies. They had come in with the avowed intention of helping us to win the War, yet they were too proud or too pig-headed to let us help them. There was tragedy in their self-sufficiency. They had to pay very dearly for their mistakes when they came up against such an intrepid and experienced fighter as

Fritz. The two Divisions to which I was temporarily attached were decimated in their first action.

It was the officers who were to blame, not the men. The men were a magnificent set of fellows, big and husky—to use their own word. They were called "Huskies." Properly led they would have been capable of anything. I should have enjoyed taking a Company of them over the top. Their officers let them down. They were too full of their own importance, too jealous that we might confuse their lack of knowledge with inefficiency.

It seemed that the higher the command, the greater the stupidity. Shortly after I joined them I gave a lecture to the officers of one of the Divisions on bombing and trench clearing, a subject I had at my finger-tips. It was outside our programme but the Brigadier asked me to do it and of course I consented. The hall was packed—but—not a single officer was present above the rank of Lieutenant. I was a Lieutenant and officers senior to that rank considered it would be *infra dig* to listen to me.

I thought it extremely amusing; the Brigadier was furious. I dined with him the following night and told him about it. Immediately after dinner he got in his car and drove down to interview the American higher command. I believe he made the sparks fly.

Our main item was a demonstration of a " Platoon in the Attack," which we carried out strictly in accordance with the official pamphlet issued on the subject. At this period of the War the platoon was considered as the principal unit of the Army. It was self-contained, consisting of four sections. A Lewis gun section, with two guns. A section of rifle grenadiers who were also bombers, and two sections of rifle and bayonet men. An army in miniature, the Lewis guns supplying covering machine-gun fire; the rifle grenadiers acting as artillery; and the riflemen making the infantry assault.

My friend Edward Holder, the "Ox," usually gave the demonstration as it was his platoon. The two platoons with which I had originally started were now separated and I had attached myself to the Ox for convenience. On the day in question our audience consisted of an American regiment. The men sat round on the grass in the form of a horseshoe, the Ox standing in the middle and explaining what was happening. First of all the attack was carried out by numbers to a whistle, the Ox from time to time stopping the advance to explain each strategical manœuvre. Afterwards a spectacular display was carried out with ball cartridges, the rifle grenadiers firing live bombs and putting up a smoke screen. The men were drilled to the minute and the result was a masterpiece of co-ordination between different arms.

The Brigadier rode up whilst the show was in progress and joined the group of officers where I was enlarging on the Ox's commentary. I was receiving a sneering reception, the general opinion being that American troops would storm their objective without bothering about such fads as covering fire and barrages, etc.

"In any case it doesn't require much training or practice to do a show like that," commented one officer.

The Brigadier was on him like a knife.

"Very well," he snapped. "I should like one of your platoons to give us a demonstration immediately."

The result was a complete fiasco. The men were willing enough but they simply did not understand what they were trying to do. I strolled round to where the Lewis gunners were stationed on one flank. They were trying to fit the magazine on to the gun upside down! The riflemen were shooting indiscriminately in every direction whilst I decided to keep as far away from the bombers as possible. I should not have been in the least surprised had there been one or two casualties.

When they had finished the General let them have it hot and strong, pointing out what would have happened had they been facing a real enemy. After that we had a somewhat better reception.

Off parade we found them a very decent set of fellows. We also made a first-hand acquaintance with the workings of the Prohibition Act. The American Army was officially Dry. Its component parts were decidedly the reverse. Our very first call was on an American Colonel in charge of a Regiment, about two thousand men. We wanted to introduce ourselves, tell him about the demonstrations we were prepared to give, and arrange when and where they were to take place.

He received us very politely. After our business had been discussed and whilst we were preparing to leave, he invited us into his bedroom. We were decidedly intrigued by the invitation and wondered what we were to see. The Colonel carefully closed the door. With an air of deepest mystery he felt under the bed and drew forth a case of whisky.

" You won't tell anyone about this ? " he enjoined as we raised our glasses.

It was the same wherever we went. They all had their private store but they were all afraid to let their companions know about it. At least that was the situation until the Officers' Club was formed.

Whence came his supplies remains a secret. One day an Officer in our Army Service Corps erected a marquee in a field and called it the Officers' Club. The Ox and I went round to visit it. There were no chairs. Just a long bar running from one end to the other behind which white-coated barmen served drinks without rest. The members, if I may use the word, stood about in groups talking and getting on with the business of consuming as much alcohol as possible in as short a time as possible.

" Whisky straights " were the order of the night.

Double tots of whisky without any soda or water to spoil the flavour. The pace was about one drink every quarter of an hour. The Ox and I were looked down on because we would not keep up and would insist on a certain amount of dilution.

Needless to relate there was plenty of argument as the evening wore on. One of the two Divisions in the neighbourhood was from the South ; the other was from the East side of New York. Someone mentioned the North and South War. It was like putting a spark in a barrel of gunpowder. In an instant they were at it hammer and tongs.

At the end of the evening we set out to help two of them home. Neither was very steady on his feet. Mine hailed from Alabama whilst the Ox's was a Yank. They were still arguing. When they reached the point of wanting to fight we left them. I put mine in a ditch on one side of the road and the Ox did the same with his on the other. We could hear them shouting at one another from some distance off. I think they were both too drunk to get to blows.

The Club did not last very long. The authorities got wind of it and closed it down. Whilst it lasted the promoter must have coined money.

One night we were invited to dinner in an American Mess. It was a very interesting experience to undergo once in a lifetime. The food consisted of stew from the Company dixie rounded off with bread and marmalade. Orinary service rations in fact. We were given Chianti to drink. I imagine a bottle was secured specially for the occasion. Most of them drank water and looked envious. During the meal we were treated to a performance by a real jazz band. It had one advantage. It precluded all possibility of any sort of conversation. We left early.

The Americans are undoubtedly a great Nation. They were raw and untrained when I saw them, but I had not the slightest doubt that they would shake down into really first-class troops under the refining influence of going under fire. I should like to have seen them in action with some of our experienced officers to advise them, provided they would allow themselves to be advised. I think they would have done well.

I was with them just over a month. Then one day when I visited the battalion Ossy informed me that there was another job waiting for me.

CHAPTER FIVE

QUIBERVILLE

AFTER nearly four years of desperate conflict the Army was beginning to run short of reinforcements. Although every effort was being made at home to keep up the supply, the demand was so great that the strain was commencing to tell. To help ease the situation the training department at G.H.Q. decided to make a grand comb out of all fit troops on the lines of communication.

Many people do not realise that for every soldier manning a trench, some fifteen people are employed in keeping him supplied with food and ammunition. This figure relates solely to transportation and the handling of stores. If the numbers employed in manufacture were included it would be very much higher. In the Air Force for instance it has been estimated that four hundred people were occupied in keeping one pilot in the air.

It will at once be seen that here was a very fruitful field for recruiting fit men for the Infantry. Not all those engaged behind the lines fell into medical categories which excluded them from the rigours of active service. Many were perfectly sound in wind and limb. These were prised out from their comfortable quarters at the Base and herded into two reinforcement camps to be trained as Infantry.

I was appointed as Adjutant of No. 2 Reinforcement Training Camp which was opened at Quiberville, some fourteen kilometres west of Dieppe on the coast. Major Baker on the Staff at G.H.Q., who had frequently visited us in connection with the training of our demonstration platoons for the American Army, was pleased to consider me eminently suitable for the post. He had been very favourably impressed with my organising and administrative ability.

Accordingly, accompanied by my servant, I arrived at Quiberville one sunny morning with instructions to report to Lieutenant-Colonel Bridcutt, Commanding. I found the Colonel in his shirt sleeves in a sea of canvas. Two thousand men and a train of lorries loaded with tents had arrived on the site chosen for the camp the day before. The Colonel was faced with the gigantic task of organising a camp, arranging all the hundred and one details relating to commissariat, etc., and getting the training programme underway. He was an ex-sergeant-major of the Coldstreams which will amply explain why such an undertaking was not beyond him. Five minutes after my arrival I, too, was in my shirt-sleeves.

For three weeks I never left the precincts of the camp. There was too much to do. Directly the Colonel found he could rely on me he left as much of the administration as possible in my hands and devoted his tremendous energy to training. But his experience and advice were always at my disposal. With him lies the credit of our success. He was a great man and deserved better luck than he received. After a month he was ordered to take over the command of a battalion in the front line. Shortly afterwards he was killed in action.

His place was taken by another man every bit as efficient as Colonel Bridcutt. He too was an ex-sergeant-major. If those two were typical examples of the pre-War soldier I can easily understand how we had such an efficient army at the outbreak of war.

Lieutenant-Colonel J. Payne originated from the Devon Regiment, where before the War he was Regimental-Sergeant-Major. At the outbreak of war he was made Captain and Adjutant in Kitchener's new army. He was awarded a D.C.M. in the South African War. During the European War he won the Military Cross and the bar to the Military Cross. As he was fifty-three years of age when war started his record is a truly magnificent one. He is also a member of His Majesty's bodyguard—a Beefeater.

Under his command I had an absolutely free hand to do as I liked. He simply did not want to be bothered with correspondence and routine matters. That was my department and he relied on me to get on with it. All he asked was efficiency. Almost his whole time was spent in training.

The official programme laid down that the men were to be turned into Infantry in six weeks. It was a stupendous task. The trainees were the opposite of volunteers. In most cases they did not want to become Infantry at all and had spent most of the War avoiding all possibility of it. Consequently there was no great willingness to learn. They simply had to be driven.

During the period I was there we had eleven murderers through the camp. They were sent out from serving life sentences at home with a chance to make good. Frequent reports had to be rendered as to their conduct. It is interesting that they gave us very little trouble.

One day when I was off duty in my hut a man knocked at the door.

" May I speak to you a minute, sir ? "

" What do you want ? " I asked sharply. " Don't you know the proper way to approach me ? "

He should have gone first to the sergeant in charge of his platoon who would have passed his request to me through the camp sergeant-major. We were obliged to be very strict in our discipline.

" Yes sir, but this is a very special private matter."

Something in his manner appealed to my sympathy and I gave him permission to speak.

" It's like this, sir," he explained. " I'm a detective in civilian life. Before the War I had occasion to arrest a man for murder. He's just been drafted into my tent and I'm afraid that if he recognises me he may do me an injury. What I want to know is, may I move to another part of the camp ? "

Needless to relate I granted his request.

I very quickly changed the Camp Sergeant-Major. The one provided by the authorities was not nearly strong enough. I insisted on having a guardsman. The one I got was ideal in every respect.

Sergeant-Major Proctor of the Irish Guards was a tall, well-built man with one of the fiercest ginger moustaches I have ever seen. It was a great asset because in reality he was extremely good-natured. A delinquent had only to catch sight of that moustache, however, and he was immediately intimidated. I never wish to have a better man to support me.

I was lucky, too, in my Orderly Room Sergeant. After we got into working order he handled all purely routine matters, leaving me free to attend to the more important correspondence. Had we tried to stick to the numbers of clerks allotted us we should have been hopelessly under-staffed. I got over the difficulty by taking a number of clerks out of the camp and putting them temporarily into the Orderly Room. Every fortnight I changed them for a fresh batch and returned the others to duty. In this way they were only delayed a fortnight in their training, and Sergeant Parker was able to get through the work of his office without difficulty. The men chosen were delighted to postpone going up the line for a fortnight ; Parker was able to close the office at a reasonable hour ; the Commanding Officer was efficiently served ; everybody was satisfied.

Another way in which I took matters into my own hands was by promoting my servant to be a sergeant. Of course he did not receive any extra pay. I merely bought some stripes and had them sewn on to his sleeve.

In this way I killed two birds with one stone. The Mess required someone extra efficient to run it. Cannon was eminently suitable. I also wanted to make him as comfortable as possible. As a sergeant he was free of the Sergeants' Mess.

"Sergeant" Cannon was an amazingly efficient fellow. He came to me one day when I was needing a servant and offered his services. From then onwards he took me in charge. It would be impossible for me to have been better looked after.

Almost his first action was to condemn my tunics as unworthy of me. I meekly promised to order a new one when I was next on leave. He told me there was no need for me to wait until then. He could arrange it immediately. He was a partner in a firm of West End tailors—Messrs. Chappell & Cannon of Sackville Street.

Cannon measured me and sent the particulars to his partner in England. In due course the clothes arrived to be tried on. After the usual business of pins and chalk they went back to be finished. Later I received the completed suit. It was perfect. I had never had such a faultless fit in my life. Chappell is in the first flight as a cutter.

Although I had to work pretty hard at first, I had plenty of leisure later on. For the first three weeks I had been hearing glowing accounts of the delightful little town situated in the bay about half a mile from the camp. One day I decided to investigate for myself.

Quiberville is a seaside resort patronised mostly by the middle class. It was the height of its season and its tiny front of some three hundred yards was packed with matrons and their families. The Mess had already secured one of the row of bathing huts, and those who had been lucky enough to go down daily already knew most of the French visitors. Before I knew where I was I found myself being introduced right and left. L'entente cordiale was very much in evidence, fostered on our side by lack of female society, on theirs by the fact that all their eligible men were fighting for their country.

Most of us bathed every day, often twice a day. A series of dances was organised in the Town Hall and we often had a cooling dip afterwards. The dances were very good fun, though of necessity conducted under the watchful eyes of the mammas and chaperones who ranged themselves solidly round the wall. No French girl is allowed the licence that happily obtains in England.

One of the most amusing fellows in the camp was a New Zealander in the Royal Engineers who was attached to us to superintend the erection of the cookhouses, etc. He conceived the brilliant idea of constructing a boat for our entertainment. He secured the necessary timber and I assisted in its construction. The work was carried out surreptitiously in an empty hut. Later we obtained the Colonel's official permission on the flimsy pretext of putting some firing targets out to sea. It was completed by then though. Not that I think the Colonel would have opposed us in any case. He was always ready to sanction any healthy amusement.

The day the last screw was put into place, we realised our stupidity. It had been quite easy to carry the timber piecemeal through the door ; it was another thing to remove the finished article. There was nothing for it but to take the hut to pieces first.

I arranged a fatigue party who carried the hull down to the water's edge. We stepped the mast and solemnly pushed off. She carried a mainsail and a foresail in addition to a pair of sculls. These were essential accessories as, having no keel, it was impossible to beat up to windward. The best we could do with our sail was to run before the wind. Her name, bravely painted on the side, was *The C3*.

She was the greatest fun apart from her usefulness. We did actually anchor the targets out at sea as promised. Mostly she was used for getting a swim in deep water. On one or two occasions we took parties of giggling French maidens for trips round the bay. But that was before the great shipwreck. Afterwards no one could be persuaded to risk their lives with us, with the single exception of Captain Lorie of the Royal Irish Rifles, a kindred spirit.

Lorie and I were alone in her when it happened. It was inclined to be choppy and the extra buffeting must have upset the caulking between the timbers. Suddenly she filled with water. We were some distance off shore. We could not take to the boats in the approved fashion because there was no boat to take to. There was nothing for it but to swim home. Fortunately we were both in Rugger outfit, a wise precaution. It was a Sunday afternoon and the promenade was crowded as we emerged from the sea like drowned rats. Shortly afterwards the excellent Cannon, having heard of the disaster, arrived with some dry clothes.

For the following two days a storm raged and we gave our toy up for lost. After it had subsided one of the men from the camp, out walking along the beach, came across the poor old *C3* half buried in sand. He reported his discovery to me and I at once fell-in a fatigue party of forty men armed with spades. The Colonel spotted them as they were marching out of the camp and wanted to know where they were going.

" Oh, they're just off for a route march, sir," I replied evasively.

" But why the spades ? "

" I thought they would give them a foretaste of what

to expect when they reach the front," I explained ingeniously.

" You're sure they've got nothing to do with that damned boat of yours ? " laughed the Colonel.

She was absolutely undamaged. We dug her out and brought her home and re-caulked her. She was as good as ever. The only effect of the storm was that we now had her entirely to ourselves. No longer was there a rush to go out in her.

They were great days. We had a lot of fun but we also did a lot of work. I was happy in that, although I could not go to the front myself, I was helping the War on by sending reinforcements. Then one day I had a telephone call from the battalion to say they had received orders to proceed up the line. The call came through at eight o'clock in the evening. By nine my resignation was in Colonel Payne's hands.

At first he tried to dissuade me. The old story. I had done my share and all that sort of thing. When he realised I was determined he did all he could to help me. He set me free immediately without waiting for official sanction from G.H.Q. He was a soldier and he understood my feelings.

The following is a copy of the report he wrote in my Record of Services.

" An extremely capable officer—has shown marked ability while officiating as Adjutant in this camp. He relinquished his position voluntarily to rejoin the Honourable Artillery Company who were reported as ' going into action.' His very cheery manner and efficient methods greatly assisted the arduous training here."

There is a postscript.

" His exploits in the C3 will never be forgotten."

I left the camp the following day with a very reluctant Cannon. He thought me completely mad. Perhaps I was. I cannot logically put down my obsession to return to the line entirely to patriotism. I have thought over it many times since without reaching a definite conclusion as to what actuated me. This I know; I knew it then. Had I remained in my soft billet whilst my Regiment was in action I should have lost my self-respect for ever. Apart from that I yearned to feel once more the thrill of " going over the top." I was destined to be disappointed.

We took train to Peronne. It was the middle of October and the weather was bitterly cold. I found it impossible to keep warm even with a blanket wrapped round me. Most of the journey I shivered violently. My head throbbed with a splitting headache. When I slept, which was in fits and starts, strange nightmares tormented my brain.

We reached our destination at two o'clock in the morning of the second day. Peronne was rail-head and the rest of the journey must be made on horseback or on foot. I had wired that I was on the way and expected to be met. No one of my battalion was at the station nor was there any message.

I left Cannon sitting on our luggage and set out to make enquiries. The town seemed deserted ; outside the station there was not a light to be seen. I walked forward without any idea where I was going. I felt sick and tired. The only thought in my mind was that I must find the battalion.

So this was Peronne. The last time I was in the line it had been many kilometres behind the German position. Now it was rail-head. It was good to be here even though I was so damnably cold. I was back in the forward area again. Soon I should find the battalion and all would be well.

I wandered on and on. Now I was clear of the town and in a country road. My footsteps faltered but still I went forward. Strange fancies filled my brain. I knew from the stars I was travelling east. If I kept on long enough I must eventually reach the front line trench. Even if I did not find my battalion I should find someone to tell me where they were.

Forward, on and on. My strength was failing now and I was not quite steady on my feet. Once or twice I stumbled ; then I fell. I picked myself laboriously up again. Even though my body was weak my mind was steadfast. I must keep on and reach the battalion.

I stumbled again ; tried to recover myself ; stepped into an abyss ; was conscious of falling down, down, down. Oblivion !

CHAPTER SIX

GERMANY

SOME passing troops found me lying unconscious in a ditch. They picked me up and packed me off to hospital. Twenty-four hours later I was back at the Base. My effort to reach the front line had failed. I had fallen a victim to the epidemic of 'flu which was raging at the time.

Fortunately I had not missed anything. The battalion had been included in the Fourth Guards Brigade which was employed as a mobile column. They were carried in an enormous train of two hundred and forty lorries, twenty-five men and a Lewis gun in each. They were attached to the First Cavalry Division. The idea was that when the cavalry succeeded in breaking through, a picked force of infantry would be available to follow up and consolidate their success. Barbed wire and innumerable trenches made the employment of cavalry ineffective and the column was never brought into use. After a month of careering about the country they were broken up. The Honourable Artillery Company were sent back to G.H.Q., where I joined them after being discharged from hospital in the beginning of November. I was sorry for their sakes that they did not get their chance ; for my own I was glad they were not employed. I should have hated to have missed a stunt of that description.

As all the world knows the Armistice was signed at eleven o'clock on the morning of the eleventh of November. We heard the news a few minutes later

264

and everyone went mad with excitement. We all visited each other's Mess and toasted Der Tag which had crowned our efforts. I am glad to be able to relate that even in those moments of delirious gratefulness that the clemency of Almighty God had spared us to see the end of the greatest struggle in history, we did not forget those of our comrades who had fallen.

The most interesting event of the day was the great privilege I was accorded of seeing the secret map kept by Operations Department showing the disposition of all the German divisions on the Western front. Opposite the Belgian Army in the north they were very few and far apart. In the south facing the Americans they were a trifle more frequent. The French were paid the compliment of having them two deep. They were densest in their desperate endeavour to prevent the victorious onrush of the British, being always three deep and in some cases four deep. I felt very proud of being a Britisher as I looked at it. There was no doubt about which of their enemies Fritz feared most.

Naturally there was great speculation about what was to happen next. For days we argued and waited. Rumour was rife as usual. At last the Second Army received definite orders to move forward to the Rhine. I was filled with envy of their good fortune. Then we heard that the Provost Marshal's command was to be augmented for service in the occupied area. Eleven of us volunteered and were accepted.

The journey through the devastated area was of immense interest. The railway engineers had achieved a marvellous work in the reconstruction of the line. Even so the train could only proceed for many miles at walking pace. The track ran over filled-in trenches and shell-holes, and for the first time since 1914 we were able to view the enemy front line without the possibility of being summarily disposed of by a sniper.

General Plumer's Headquarters was at Spa, just

short of the promised land. Here we reported to Lieutenant-Colonel Percy C. Laurie, the Deputy Provost-Marshal of the Second Army. The Colonel singled me out for special service with him, the others being drafted to various Divisions and Corps.

I remained at Spa for a week and then, one memorable night, I was despatched with two other fellows to Duren. At last we were in Germany and, with the exception of a skeleton advanced guard, ahead of all British troops. It was decidedly exhilarating to walk about amongst our conquered enemies. I had a very distinct feeling of superiority.

At Duren I was made responsible for the issue of all passes to Germans wishing to travel from the area we were occupying to other parts of Germany. I was perhaps the best man for the job and the worst. It depends on the point of view. The best in that, hating the Huns as I did, I examined each application that came before me with the most precise and meticulous care. Being unable to understand a single word of German I was obliged to rely on an interpreter. The result was that pleadings and entreaties went for nothing. They lose most of their rhetorical force when briefly translated. The worst in that I held up all communication with unoccupied Germany for ten days ; at least all official communication. I have no doubt that vast numbers of people ignored my ruling and travelled just the same, without the necessary passport. I only issued a total of eleven passes altogether.

After ten days they relieved me of the job and handed it over to someone less ruthless who had the added advantage of knowing what he was doing. A week or so later I had occasion to visit the newly opened Passampt. Some ten or twelve interpreters and a staff of over a hundred clerks were hard at work doing the task to which I had given a few minutes each morning. I often roar with laughter when I think of it.

That was in Cologne to which we moved after six days. Here I took up my residence in the Dom Hotel opposite the Cathedral. I had a suite of rooms on the first floor consisting of a bedroom, a bathroom and a sitting-room which I shared with another fellow.

We arrived in Cologne before the tail of the German Army had finished crossing the Rhine. They were still trailing over the Hohenzollern Bridge. By the sides of the roads over which they had passed, broken waggons, discarded equipment, and unneeded cannon marked their passage. The men themselves were anything but downcast. For a beaten Army they were remarkably cheerful. They were going home where in most cases they had never expected to see home again.

Soon after our arrival in the city I was allotted a new job. My instructions were to organise some motor-boat police patrols on the Rhine. This was really a job for the Navy, but owing to the Rhine debouching on to the sea through a neutral country, they were obliged to bring their M.L.'s through the canals of Belgium. This would take some time and until they arrived I was to carry on.

The first thing to do was to organise my fleet. The first step was to call at the bureau which the Burgomaster had arranged for the convenience of his conquerors. The opening of this bureau was a masterly move illustrating the foresight and thoroughness of the German people. The Cologne Council wished to prevent any possibility of looting so they anticipated it by meeting the first British contingent with the news that they could have anything they needed for the asking. All it was necessary to do was to call at the Bureau and sign a requisition form. The article demanded, whether desk, piece of furniture, stationery, motor-car or anything else was delivered at any address stated. The same routine produced billets and offices. It was a a wonderful system which avoided all unnecessary fuss and confusion.

I required eight motor-boats. An official was detailed who conducted me along the river-side so that I could make my choice. Naturally I chose the biggest, fastest and best for myself, but all were good. They have to be powerful on the Rhine where the current flows so much faster than the Thames.

Stationed at each end of our area was a Company of men whose job was to examine the passes of all craft entering or leaving the British bridge-head. I allotted two craft to each. The remainder patrolled up and down to control traffic crossing from one bank to the other. This system obtained until the arrival of the M.L.'s in the New Year.

The A.P.M. of Cologne was Major Ralph Maude, a younger brother of the famous Cyril. He had achieved a tremendous popularity at Amiens which he had policed for the greater part of the War. His star acquired an even brighter lustre at Cologne where his great gift of firmness tempered with tact had so much more scope. He was absolutely the right man in the right job and as head of the British police he had a large share in the example of how-to-behave-when-on-top which the British troops showed the rest of the world. In this he was helped considerably by the exemplary conduct of the Guards Division garrisoning the City.

He struck up a firm friendship with me right from the first and after a time I went nearly everywhere with him. He begged me from Colonel Laurie, and as my position as head of the motor-boat controls was really a sinecure—the job ran itself—I was duly transferred. My duties with Major Maude were very light. He used to refer to me as his big bodyguard. He was little more than five feet. When he went abroad I travelled with him in the car. We were never once molested, so I had no occasion to go into action. In short I had a very easy time.

There was one job, however, which I was never allowed to neglect. Punctually at eleven o'clock each morning I had to burst into the Major's room regardless of whom he might be interviewing. With a punctilious salute I would make a daily announcement.

"I have that special report you asked for, sir."

If the Major had someone of importance with him he would glance at his watch, appear to hesitate, then apparently reach a decision. He had the family instinct for acting.

"Very well, Pollard. Take it to my private sitting-room. I'll join you in a few minutes."

It was wonderful camouflage. The private and special report consisted merely of a bottle and two glasses. But we never missed.

We messed at the house of one Baron von Guillaume. He was a millionaire and he had a wonderful place. The rooms we used were oak-panelled and hung with rare tapestries. Nor was our food below the standard of our accommodation. Colonel Bailey, the head of the Navy and Army Canteen, messed with us. Through his influence we managed extremely well.

I visited as much as possible of the occupied area whilst I had the chance. Bonn, Coblentz, Euskirchen gave me some slight insight into different types of German workers. Everywhere I went I was struck by the healthy vigour of the many children. There were no signs of decadence about them. I could not help thinking forward to the time when they were grown up and able to raise their voices in deciding the destiny of their Nation. Would they call for peace or revenge?

They are grown up now and banded together in a mighty organisation. So far the Treaty imposed on them has prevented them from arming themselves. So far the reorganisation of their own affairs at home has debarred them from seriously turning their attention to their relationships with their neighbours and late antagonists. But the time is not very far distant when they will demand a hearing. They will have to receive attention. The call of robust youth cannot be ignored. They will want to be unshackled, to be acquitted of the sins of their fathers. It is up to the statesmen of the leading nations of the world to investigate their claims before a crisis is precipitated with inevitable bloodshed.

Christmas came and passed. The general conversation centred more and more round demobilisation. Colonel Laurie went on leave and returned with the news that he had been appointed to a position at Scotland Yard. He stayed only long enough to hand over to Lieutenant-Colonel Mellor and then departed for good. His police experience stood him in good stead and he is now well known as the popular head of the Mounted branch.

I began seriously to think of my own future. My inclination tended towards a commission in the Regular Army, but my wife was opposed to the idea and I reluctantly abandoned it.

At the beginning of February I went on my final leave. By the kindness of Colonel Mellor who was crossing on the same day I travelled with him to Boulogne by car. It took us three days, and as we went right through the area where the fighting had been thickest the journey was particularly interesting. A detour through Ginchy where my brother was killed enabled me to make a search for his grave, but without avail. He is one of the many whose bodies were never traced.

I spent my leave looking for a suitable job. I could of course have gone back to my stool with the Alliance Assurance Company, but after four and a half years of open-air life the prospect did not appeal. My preliminary investigations were fruitless, but, at the same time, showed me some of the difficulties which the Army would experience in being re-absorbed as civilians. I decided that the sooner I got out of khaki the better.

I returned to Cologne and at once put in my papers. A week later, on the 23rd February, 1919, I ceased to be a unit in the biggest, greatest, and most efficient Army the British Empire has ever put in the field. But I knew in my heart, and I know it now, if ever my King and Country have a further need for my services, I will gladly offer them.

EPILOGUE

THIRTEEN years have passed since I was demobilised. For me they have been years of many ups and downs. I left the Army full of the confidence of youth, believing that the success which had attended me through the War would be of advantage to me in the Peace. I was made quickly to understand how small a connection there was between the two.

Like many thousands of others I had to start again from the beginning ; not once but several times. By this statement I am not casting any reflection on my employers. My difficulties have been mostly psychological, due no doubt to a change of outlook influenced by the War. My Insurance job was open for me. I felt at one time that I should be obliged to go back to it. They had been decent enough to pay me my salary regularly and I was under an obligation. Mr. Owen Morgan Owen, who was at that time in charge, quickly eased my mind.

"Consider we have been paying you a premium to insure ourselves against the results of an enemy invasion," he said. "You need not return to us if you do not wish to, although we should be very pleased to have you."

I did not accept his offer but resigned. In accepting my resignation the Directors voted me a year's salary as a gift. I consider their action a most generous one.

Since then I have been in several different positions, including a short service commission in the Royal Air Force. Now I am a novelist with three published books to my credit.

Life has been to me like a game of Snakes and Ladders. Sometimes a cast of the dice has carried me on to prosperity with a rush ; at others, I have been thrust back to zero. I am at present on a ladder which I believe will carry me to my goal.

My marriage was a failure. After five years my wife divorced me. The circumstances which led up to such a climax are naturally not for the public eye. The result was that, deprived of my lodestar, I went completely off my course. For two or three years I did every conceivable damned silly thing imaginable. Then some latent spark of commonsense within me whispered, " Why be such a fool ? "

I put on the brake and began to regain my self-control. My luck still held. I met and married my present wife. She is the perfect mate. We have now been married for six years and are greater lovers than on the day we were first joined together.

More important still, we are friends. To her never-failing sympathy, courage, and help, I owe the fact that I am a better man to-day than I have ever been in my life before.

Some years ago she presented me with the following verse, which I look at every day, and which never fails to help me square my shoulders to face adversity :

BOUND TO WIN

Take this honey for the bitterest cup ;
There is no failure save in giving up,
No real fall so long as one still tries,
For seeming setbacks make the strong man wise,
There's no defeat, in truth, save from within,
Unless you're beaten there you're bound to win.

INDEX

A

Abbeville, 166, 201
Alliance Assurance Co. Ltd., 21, 270, 272
American Army, 241, 245, 246-253
Ancre, the, 168
Armoury House, 23, 236
Arras, 19, 203, 224, 230
Aspinall, Colonel, G.S.O., 63rd Division, 20, 228
Aveley, 27
Ayres, " Tubby," 134

B

Bailey, Colonel, N.A.A.F.I., 269
Baillescourt Farm, 186
Bailleul (near Kemmel), 35, 37
Bailleul (near Arras), 203
Baker, Major, G.H.Q. Training Staff, 255
Barrett, Artie, 201
Beaucourt, 168
Beauregard Dovecote, 194
Billiken, 168, 179
Boulogne, 99, 245
Bouvigny Wood, 138
Boyle, Lieutenant - Colonel Ernest, 51, 53, 60, 64, 69, 77, 78, 82, 84, 132, 136, 137, 149, 154, 164, 171, 177, 178
Bridcutt, Lieutenant-Colonel, 255
Brother, my, 25, 148

Brown, Lce-Corpl. " Buster," 31
Bryan, Captain Sterry, 177, 181
Burgess, Sergeant, 183, 189

C

C3, the, 260
Calonne, 141, 147, 149
Cannon, " Sergeant," 258
Chaland, Ernest, 26, 31, 32, 34, 45, 65, 69, 74, 78, 81, 91, 92
Chappell & Cannon, 258
Cologne, 267
Cooper, Lieutenant-Colonel P. C., 231

D

Daily Express, 44
Davis, " Duggie," 49, 55, 56, 88, 135
Denbigh, Colonel the Earl of Denbigh and Desmond, C.V.O., A.D.C., 26, 237, 240
Dickebushe, 64, 71
Douai, 213, 215
Douglas, Major (Bt. Lt.-Col.), M.C., D.S.O., O.B.E., M.C., 25, 91
Duren, 266

E

Ellis, Captain " Ted," 133, 157
Ellis, " Skipper," 135

275